HODGES UNIVERSITY

P9-DCL-341

Interactional Coaching

Interactional coaching is a powerful, one-to-one learning approach, used successfully for over fifteen years, that enables executives to make the choices that work for them. Drawing on existential philosophy, psychotherapy and business theory, interactional coaching uses innovative techniques to help clients identify their best possible choices and effectively put them into practice.

Featuring numerous case studies, which integrate theoretical principles with practical tools, *Interactional Coaching* illustrates:

- coaching for vision and other time-related issues
- coaching in the personal dimension
- coaching interactional strategy and skills
- coaching conflicts and dilemmas
- coaching creativity and communication
- coaching leadership and managerial expertise.

Interactional Coaching: Choice-Focused Learning at Work is essential reading for anyone interested in a new, comprehensive approach to helping coachees develop the self-knowledge and interpersonal skills necessary for achievement in today's workplace.

Michael Harvey is a business psychologist and founder of interactional coaching, based in London, UK.

Essential Coaching Skills and Knowledge
Series Editors: Gladeana McMahon,
Stephen Palmer & Averil Leimon

The **Essential Coaching Skills and Knowledge** series provides an accessible and lively introduction to key areas in the developing field of coaching. Each title in the series is written by leading coaches with extensive experience and has a strong practical emphasis, including illustrative vignettes, summary boxes, exercises and activities. Assuming no prior knowledge, these books will appeal to professionals in business, management, human resources, psychology, counselling and psychotherapy, as well as students and tutors of coaching and coaching psychology.

www.routledgementalhealth.com/essential-coaching-skills

Titles in the series:

Essential Business Coaching
Averil Leimon, François Moscovici & Gladeana McMahon

Achieving Excellence in Your Coaching Practice: How to Run a Highly Successful Coaching Business
Gladeana McMahon, Stephen Palmer & Christine Wilding

A Guide to Coaching and Mental Health: The Recognition and Management of Psychological Issues
Andrew Buckley & Carole Buckley

Essential Life Coaching Skills
Angela Dunbar

The Coaching Relationship: Putting People First
Stephen Palmer & Almuth McDowall

101 Coaching Strategies and Techniques
Edited by Gladeana McMahon & Anne Archer

Group and Team Coaching: The Essential Guide
Christine Thornton

Coaching Women to Lead
Averil Leimon, François Moscovici & Helen Goodier

Developmental Coaching: Life Transitions and Generational Perspectives
Edited by Stephen Palmer & Sheila Panchal

Cognitive Behavioural Coaching in Practice: An Evidence Based Approach
Edited by Michael Neenan & Stephen Palmer

Brief Coaching: A Solution Focused Approach
Chris Iveson, Evan George & Harvey Ratner

Interactional Coaching: Choice-Focused Learning at Work
Michael Harvey

Interactional Coaching

Choice-Focused Learning at Work

Michael Harvey

Routledge
Taylor & Francis Group

LONDON AND NEW YORK

First published 2012
by Routledge
27 Church Road, Hove, East Sussex BN3 2FA

Simultaneously published in the USA and Canada
by Routledge
711 Third Avenue, New York NY 10017

*Routledge is an imprint of the Taylor & Francis Group,
an informa business*

© 2012 Michael Harvey

All rights reserved. No part of this book may be reprinted or
reproduced or utilised in any form or by any electronic, mechanical,
or other means, now known or hereafter invented, including
photocopying and recording, or in any information storage or
retrieval system, without permission in writing from the publishers.

Trademark notice: Product or corporate names may be trademarks or
registered trademarks, and are used only for identification and
explanation without intent to infringe.

British Library Cataloguing in Publication Data
A catalogue record for this book is available from the British Library

Library of Congress Cataloging in Publication Data
Harvey, Michael Denis Bagenal, 1952-
  Interactional coaching : choice-focused learning at work /
Michael Harvey.
  — 1st ed.
    p. cm.
Includes bibliographical references and index.
1. Personal coaching.   I. Title.
  BF637.P36H378 2012
  158.3—dc23

2011038294

ISBN: 978-0-415-61473-3 (hbk)
ISBN: 978-0-415-61472-6 (pbk)
ISBN: 978-0-203-12444-4 (ebk)

Typeset in New Century Schoolbook
by RefineCatch Limited, Bungay, Suffolk
Paperback cover design by Lisa Dynan

MIX
Paper from
responsible sources
FSC® C004839
www.fsc.org

Printed and bound in Great Britain by
TJ International Ltd, Padstow, Cornwall

Dedication

To Helen, Frances, James and Patrick

About the author

Michael Harvey is an executive coach and business psychologist, whose previous career roles include university teacher, corporate manager, media entrepreneur and psychotherapist. Since the mid-1990s, he's coached executives from many different types of organizations, throughout the UK and Europe. He has a first-class degree in psychology from London University and Master's degrees in psychotherapy, organizational psychology and English Literature. He lives and works in London and can be contacted at michael@interactionalcoaching.com.

These four questions also say something of my own journey as coach over the past decade and a half. In addition, they represent a fair summary of some of the issues I've tried to address in this book, so let me give you an indication of how I would answer them:

1 *What is executive coaching?* It is an adaptable form of one-to-one learning. My model, interactional coaching, aims to understand an executive's unique situation, clarify the choices and help him to achieve them by focusing on the most important interactions.
2 *What can interactional coaching do for me?* It aims to help clients interact more effectively with others at work, which often means helping them interact better with themselves. How they do this has a lot to do with how they interact with time, so identifying and working with the client's past experiences and future goals are also central to this approach.
3 *How does interactional coaching work?* It works by focusing on the choices that executives make – and don't make – and their ability to put these into practice. It has many different applications in the workplace, including developing leadership, self-confidence, communication skills and creativity.
4 *What is different about it?* It is a highly integrated approach that is very practical, uses a wide range of techniques and yet is theoretically consistent. It draws on existential philosophy, psychology and business theory to focus on the importance of choice-making at work and in life.

This book is really an extension of these answers and the questions that prompted them, as you might expect of a form of learning that fundamentally consists of a dialogue with its clients. For the first time, this book offers a comprehensive introduction to the practice and theory of interactional coaching, as it has developed over the past 15 years of working with many different types of executive in many different organizations.

Who is this book for?

I hope everyone who is interested in coaching can get something from this book, including practitioners, sponsors of

Preface

A history in four questions

What is executive coaching? When I began my career as a coach in the middle of the 1990s, I was often asked this question by potential clients. I had reached coaching by several routes. From a career as a corporate manager, I had gone on to become a media businessman, before training as a psychotherapist and organizational psychologist. For me, these diverse strands of experience seemed to come together quite naturally, as I began to work one-to-one with executives on the challenges and opportunities facing them. It was not surprising, however, that it took a while for this new form of learning to become well known in organizations.

By the end of the 1990s, the initial question that clients tended to raise had changed into: I've heard of coaching but what can it do for me exactly? A few years later, the line of enquiry had shifted again, this time to: How does your kind of coaching work? Nowadays, as the number of coaching approaches increases, this question is often accompanied by another, namely: How do you differ from other coaches?

In a sense, the journey of executive coaching over the past two decades can be traced in the development of these four questions. From an obscure activity pioneered by a handful of practitioners, executive coaching has developed into a diverse, multibillion dollar, worldwide practice that, in one way or another, touches the lives of hundreds of thousands of people at work every day.

Contents

coaching, HR professionals and line managers. It should be relevant to the increasing number of people at work receiving coaching, engaging in coaching skills training or using some form of coaching in their everyday jobs. Those who may have heard of coaching but are not sure what it can do for them can also benefit from this text.

What is the book's content?

Part 1

Part 1 introduces the theory and practice of interactional coaching. The first chapter outlines the situation of the modern executive and how interactional coaching relates to this. It describes the concepts of the interactional self and the centrality of choice in working situations and everyday life. In Chapter 2 we turn to an in-depth case study, a practical example of interactional coaching in action, which is followed by a description of the unique techniques, methods and theoretical principles that guide this practice in Chapter 3. The Achievement Matrix, a dynamic nine-stage model of the coaching process, is outlined in Chapter 4.

Part 2

In Part 2 we move on to specific coaching purposes. Chapter 5 explores helping clients to develop their personal vision and professional goals. Chapter 6 examines how to help coachees develop their self-knowledge, personality awareness and self-analytical ability. Chapter 7 looks at how to analyse the coachee's most important relationships at work, using such techniques as interactional mapping.

Part 3

Part 3 explores the time dimension of coaching. Chapter 8 focuses on how to coach transitions, major changes of role or organizational context in which the client is called on to bridge the gap between the past and the present. In Chapter 9 we look at managing ambiguity and uncertainty, a vivid challenge in many professional environments but also a potential opportunity.

Part 4

Part 4 is concerned with coaching in the personal dimension. In Chapter 10 we explore the crucial issue of coaching final choices and dilemmas, when coachees are focused on difficult, sometimes agonizing, decisions. Then in Chapter 11 we look at the issue of self-confidence, which also can have a dramatic impact on the careers of executives. Chapter 12 examines action and inaction and outlines effective methods for overcoming the obstacles that can frustrate coachees' attempts to put their choices into practice.

Part 5

In Part 5 we move into the dimension of others and interactional coaching's special emphasis on developing practical skills, when these are necessary for a coachee's success. Chapter 13 covers interpersonal competence, the ability to work productively with colleagues and other stakeholders to achieve one's goals. Chapter 14 shows how to coach practical communication skills that inform, engage and persuade others. In Chapter 15 we illustrate another important aspect of organizational life – conflict – and how coaching can help to resolve it using existentially informed principles.

Part 6

Part 6 focuses on leadership, one of the most popular of coaching purposes and an issue that is central to the interactional approach's concern with the consequences of choice. In Chapter 16 we look at the interactional theory of leadership biases and how leaders in challenging situations can be helped to overcome them. Chapter 17 reviews effective ways of helping clients to develop management expertise, without crossing the border between coaching and formal training.

Part 7

Further coaching purposes are described in this final part of the book. Chapter 18 looks at how to coach creativity and help clients to manage innovation, while Chapter 19 explores another issue that is extremely relevant to today's organizations – stress. In Chapter 20 we focus on handling relapses and setbacks in coaching, as well as the surprising ways in which apparent failure can turn into success.

Conclusion

Chapter 21 concludes the book with a deeper look at the practical and personal qualities required for coaching in the interactional style. The references and index can be found at the end of this section.

Acknowledgements

Finally, I'd like to thank all those who have helped me in the writing of this book, including my clients, from whom I have learnt so much over the years. I particularly want to thank my family and my friends for their curiosity, feedback and patience. Special thanks go to my colleagues, especially Ismail Asmall for supporting me through the early stages of the book, and Ernesto Spinelli for his wise words of advice. Let me also express my gratitude to the series editors and to Kate Hawes, Joanne Forshaw, Jane Harris and Erasmis Kidd at Routledge. It goes without saying that any mistakes in the book are my own.

Michael Harvey
July 2011

Part 1

Interactional coaching in theory and practice

Introduction to interactional coaching: Coaching the choice business

Let me introduce you to five people:

- Julia is a banker whose career seems to be going off the rails. 'I'm a hopeless case,' she says nervously, 'I don't know what I want any more.' Her manager is concerned that her state of mind may lead to losses for the bank.
- Alan is an experienced IT manager in an international media company who has been passed over for promotion for the third time. 'They say I don't have the necessary interpersonal skills but I'm 45. I'm not going to change the way I communicate with people now, am I?'
- Sangita is struggling to make the transition to her new management role in a government agency. She is being asked to make major cost-savings but is unable to come up with a strategy. 'My job used to be black and white,' she complains, 'now it's all greys. I don't know how to deal with that.'
- Gerry is a senior consultant who suffers terrible losses in confidence. He feels he's being exploited by his company but can't make up his mind if he wants to fight back.
- Lenny is CEO of a music company who is desperate to succeed in his first major leadership role. But the choices he is making about the direction of the company are going down badly with his staff and his management team. The result is that some of his best people are leaving and his place at the top is becoming increasingly precarious.

We'll meet these clients again in the course of this book: Julia, in some depth, in the next chapter, Sangita in Chapter 9, Gerry in Chapter 11, Alan in Chapter 13 and Lenny in Chapter 16. But for the moment let's consider what these very different executives have in common. They all seem to be trying to make the best possible choices for themselves, their colleagues and their customers. But the choices they are making are evidently not working. They either don't know what they want or don't know how to achieve it, all of which leads to powerful emotions: anxiety, doubt, frustration, anger and even despair. Their situations are critical, for themselves and their organizations, which means that helping them is all the more urgent – welcome to the world of interactional coaching!

Interactional coaching is a new, practical, one-to-one learning approach designed to help executives make the choices that are right for them and achieve what they want at work. As we'll see, it is an exceptionally adaptable form of coaching that is effective across a wide range of coaching applications and purposes. Developed over 15 years' work with many different types of executive, it differs from many other models of coaching in three respects. First, it combines extensive business experience with psychological expertise in an integrated approach. Second, it uses an exceptionally wide range of techniques and methods, ranging from open dialogue to strategic development and practical coaching around communication and interpersonal skills. Third, it has a unique theoretical focus around choice, defining human reality as 'choice-making in interaction'. In this it draws on the powerful, insightful philosophy of life, which is existential thinking, as well as other sources in psychotherapy, psychology and management studies.

In this chapter, we look in more detail at the significance of choice in the workplace and in life and at the concept of the interactional self that underlies this coaching approach. I also want to clarify the goals of interactional coaching and how it differentiates itself from other models of coaching. First, though, let's examine the role of the modern executive and the way coaching has developed to support it.

Coaching and the executive today

To be an executive today is to be in the choice business. One definition of an executive has always been an employee who is empowered to make a range of choices in an organization, as opposed to other employees who make different types of contribution. But the decision-making of contemporary executives is aimed at providing their customers and clients with what they want in the most competitive, interconnected global economy in history. This involves making crucial choices about every aspect of their organization, from strategy to personnel, from product development to marketing and distribution. These choices may well determine the success or failure of an enterprise, so the pressure to get them right is probably greater than ever before.

Some of the pressure on today's executives stems from the free market revolution of the 1980s. This period deregulated many traditional industries, privatized others and downsized middle management, making the private sector more competitive and the public sector more market-orientated (Leimon et al., 2005). A major effect of this was that, for many, 'work' was transformed into 'performance'. Suddenly a much wider range of managerial competences and interpersonal skills was required by executives than the more sedate, hierarchical organizations of the past had demanded. Work as performance implies a change in the concept of time. For example, the long-term 'job for life' culture of many twentieth-century firms, where seniority was a major criterion of status, has given way to the short-term, job-switching culture of today, where you are only as good as your last performance review. Executives, once seen as bureaucrats or semi-anonymous cogs in a corporate machine, are now performers, on stage, in full view, pushed and pushing to be at their very best and evaluated by a host of performance-management systems that determine rewards and punishment. And when economic boom gives way to recession, the stakes get even higher and the consequences of poor performance become more serious.

At the same time, much of the modern pressure to achieve comes from executives themselves. They are well aware of the responsibility they have to themselves to make the best of the opportunities with which they are presented. In general, they also recognize the responsibilities to their employers, colleagues, customers and their families and friends that their roles involve. Executives now also have a huge range of choices to make about their careers and lifestyles. Whereas their parents may have had one job in one career, today's executives could be looking at several jobs in several careers, searching for a way to balance the exhilarating but furious demands of work with the possibilities of life, family and leisure.

Over the past two decades, the practice of executive coaching has developed in order to help executives deal with this vast new array of choices, pressures and opportunities. Virtually unknown in the 1980s, executive coaching is now a multibillion dollar, worldwide industry practised by tens of thousands of coaches and used by over 80% of organizations in the UK (Chartered Institute of Personnel and Development, 2010). Agile, multipurpose, capable of changing its content and structure to deal with many different applications, it has developed out of sources as diverse as management consultancy, sports coaching and psychotherapy to become an extraordinarily effective form of workplace learning.

Practicality, client-focus and adaptability are also at the heart of interactional coaching. Its aim is to help clients like Julia, Gerry, Alan, Sangita and Lenny to make the choices that are right for them in the unique situations in which they find themselves. It is a practical approach that draws strength from its theoretical focus on the centrality of choice-making not only in work but also in every aspect of life, so it will be useful to look at this in a little more depth. For interactional coaching, the person is a complex, interactional self encountering the world through different stages of choice, from strategizing to action. In other words, it is not only executives who are in the choice business, we all are.

The choice focus

'To be is to choose oneself', wrote Jean-Paul Sartre (1958: 440). This statement forms the starting point for the interactional approach. In some ways, it may seem obvious that the big decisions we make in our lives determine our identity. One of the founders of existential thinking, Soren Kierkegaard (1992), pointed out over a century and a half ago that our choices about what job we take or who we live with are crucial to who we are, which is why these choices are often so difficult to make. In our era of unprecedented choice this is even more true, as we routinely make decisions about our work, lifestyle, religion, politics, sexuality and even physical appearance that would have been unthinkable to previous generations.

For existential-phenomenological philosophy, from which interactional coaching draws a good deal of its theoretical inspiration, the idea of choice goes even further. It implies that as humans we have no set nature or essence, as defined by religion, science or society. We are who we choose to be and exist in a continuous act of choosing. As Sartre (1958: 463) put it: 'We choose the world . . . by choosing ourselves.'

This doesn't mean that we have a totally free choice. We make our choices out of the materials that have been given to us in the past and in the present, such as culture, family and even biological constitution. These givens are not in our control but what we make of them is. Nor does our existence as choice-makers mean that every choice we make is conscious in the sense of a clear, rational weighing up of the pros and cons. On the contrary, choices can often be made emotionally or in the heat of action. Some choices we are fully aware of, some we are half-aware of and others we are hardly aware of at all. Indeed, it is often the choices we make without fully knowing it that are the most crucial in shaping our lives.

Choice is essentially a perception of difference, or an interaction of possibilities, which is why Sartre (1958: 462) said that 'choice and consciousness are one and the same thing'. Our ability as humans to perceive, feel and imagine differences, and to reflect on them, creates the new possibilities and new interactions that are a feature of our constantly changing worlds. One of the most powerful of these interactions is the relationship between what we want and what we don't want. Desire is already a kind of choice, a weighing up of possibilities that we may have little control over, but as we start to focus more intensively on the competition between desires, choice becomes a more conscious act of interpretation. We have started with a possibility and ended with a conclusion, a choice about the meaning of something. We turn through these interpretations continuously, perhaps hundreds of times in an hour.

In a wider sense, choice can be said to underwrite human society, through our laws, morality and politics. Historically, the struggle for political freedom has aimed at giving more people in society greater choices about how they are governed and by whom. The law focuses on the proper exercise of choices within a given legal code and assumes that infringements of this code are freely made choices and as such are liable to punishment. Similarly the notion of individual morality rests on the conviction that we are all responsible for our actions and our choices and that these ultimately may define our value as human beings.

But choice can be a double-edged sword. Because we are free, we have no guarantees about who we are or what is right or wrong in any situation. This leads to anxiety, which Kierkegaard (1980: 61) calls 'the dizziness of freedom'. Our ability to see that things can always be different is at the heart of our creativity and intellectual power but it can create a perpetual sense of unease. In extreme forms, anxiety can seriously limit what we can achieve. Interactional coaching is often about helping people deal with the fact that some uncertainty is inevitable and, viewed in the right light, can be a positive and productive force in work and life.

The choice cycle

Ultimately the choices that have most impact on others and ourselves are those that are turned into actions. In this sense, the destiny of choice is action, although choice has many other states, moods and realities. In order to clarify this process of choosing, interactional coaching uses a three-stage model called the choice cycle. The choice cycle emphasizes that choice-making is a totality, a complex trans-formation of a possibility into a concrete reality. It can be summed up in three words: possibilizing, probabilizing and actualizing.

The first stage of the choice cycle is the possibilizing stage. This is where one tries to identify the choices that might be applicable in any situation; it is the pre-choice stage where possibility is strongest and options abound. It is also the stage where trying to identify what you want and don't want is most needed. This can be an exciting or an anxiety-provoking stage, as it has no clearly defined structure.

The second stage is about probabilizing, a narrowing down of possibilities in the light of the human and material resources that are available and what can realistically be achieved or how much risk can be taken. This is the selection stage, where a final decision is made between options and where the challenge of choice can be acute.

The final stage of the choice cycle is about action, without which choosing is empty. Putting the chosen course of action into practice is not necessarily a single action but a series of actions requiring further choices. This implementation phase is the finalization of the cycle.

We'll see this model at work throughout many of the different purposes of interactional coaching. Regarded as a purely cognitive or emotional process it describes the act of interpretation, a possibility that ends as a conclusion rather than a specific action. In a more complex form, it makes up the Achievement Matrix, a model that helps to illuminate some of the changes that occur in coaching and guide the client towards achieving her goals. This is explained fully in Chapter 4.

The interactional self

As we've suggested, at the core of the interactional coaching model is the idea that as human beings we are choice-makers in interaction. In part, the interactional self implies that our thoughts, feelings and behaviours are not separable entities but part of a constantly interweaving reality. We are not minds versus bodies, as conventional dualistic thinking suggests, but minds *and* bodies, thoughts *and* emotions, contemplation *and* action. The interactional self also suggests that as humans we have no choice but to create value for ourselves and others. We are our own producers, out of the materials that are to hand, and our greatest creation is ourselves. We can analyse this self-choosing, value-creating process in terms of three types of interaction: our interactions with time, our interactions with ourselves and our interactions with others.

The self in time

Let's start with time, the first of the three dimensions of the interactional self. To say that a person is defined by the way she relates to time, especially the future, may seem strange at first sight. We perhaps think of ourselves as living in a present that comes out of the past, but for existential theory it is truer to say that our present comes out of our future (Heidegger, 1962). We are forward-facing, in part because we are motivated by desires that can only be fulfilled in the future, even if the future is measured in seconds. Throughout our lives we develop goals, ambitions, plans and projects and other trajectories to the future, all of which constitute much of who we are. Some people plan extensively, whereas others will define themselves by their refusal to plan ahead: either way, much of our identity at any point will be coloured by a journey towards an imagined future.

Change the future and we change the meaning of the present and possibly our interpretation of the past. Imagine you are thinking about an exciting project at work: you are enthusiastic, energetic; you are 'looking forward to' it. Suddenly you hear that the project has been cancelled: your mood drops, you feel angry, disappointed, even mildly depressed. Perhaps you think of leaving your job. The past year of struggling to get approval for the project now seems a complete waste of time, a betrayal even. Your present, in the sense of your day-to-day job and surroundings, hasn't changed an iota, but it feels totally different, as does your immediate past. And all of this is because of changes to an event in the future.

The past can also have a major influence on our identity. Pride in past achievements, for example, can spur us on to further ambitions, just as past failures may make us want to catch up for lost time. But sometimes the threat of change may make it attractive to retreat into the past or try to hang on to the present at any cost. Indeed, a strong attachment to the past may exert a powerful influence over the way we choose our future.

The self with itself

The second major aspect of the self is the personal dimension: the way we choose to interact with ourselves. Our interpretation of who we are plays a crucial role in our ability to achieve fulfilment. Beliefs, values, talents, even personality preferences are all, to some extent, aspects of ourselves that we choose to accept or change. Growing up is often a process of moving away from the givens of our birth and early life towards our own unique identity. Much is invented for us by factors beyond our control but how we re-invent these characteristics is what counts. For example, for some people having an introvert personality is something they happily accept, whereas others may be determined to change this and become more gregarious and outgoing. For one person, being born in a working class environment is embraced with pride and commitment through their life; for another, it is an inheritance they dedicate themselves to changing through social mobility or economic advancement.

The extent to which we are able to reflect on our values, thoughts and feelings is also a very significant aspect of the self. The ability to analyse our motives and beliefs and understand what lies behinds our emotions has a significant bearing on our capacity to make the choices that are right for us. Unless we can bring these 'pre-reflective' thoughts, feelings, memories and desires to the surface, it may be difficult to make informed decisions.

The self with others

The third interaction of the self is interpersonal. As humans we live in a world that is textured and contoured by the people with whom we share our lives, directly or indirectly. To be human is to be in a social, inter-subjective world, from our earliest moments onwards (Merleau-Ponty, 1962). Relating to others is especially relevant at work. Organizations are dense social networks, teeming with connections and interconnections. Who you relate to in your work and how you relate to them will go a long way to defining what you get out of an organization and what it gets out of you. Your main interactors will evaluate, reward and recognize your contribution and to this extent hold the key to your ability to achieve what you want.

However, it is worth repeating that the power of choice does not imply that we can be anything that we want. We have the right to choose to attempt to achieve anything – especially the impossible – but we always make choices in situations that are not wholly of our own making. How we deal with the factors we haven't chosen in any project – including many of our own capacities and talents – is often the determinant of success. Absolute freedom is a myth, therefore, but so is absolute unfreedom. You might say we live between freedom and fate. Even in the most difficult circumstances we always have some kind of choice, however minimal. This inalienable ability to interpret our situation can be called categorical choice. It is part of the charter of being human and a source of some of our greatest creativity, adaptability and achievement.

Choice as organizational leadership

Leadership of an organization is one of the powerful manifestations of human choice-making, in terms of the scope and quantity of the decisions that leaders make and the consequences of these decisions on other people. Many managerial tasks such as strategy, recruitment, delegation, innovation and marketing also revolve around different types of decision-making. In fact, organizations should be seen as theatres of choice. We may tend to think of them as fixed and steady and perhaps as monolithic as the buildings that some of them occupy. In reality, organizations are in a constant process of choosing themselves and their reasons for being, selecting their core products and services, their brand identity, their geographical location, their public stance, and so on.

Even the apparently impromptu or spontaneous behaviour that employees exhibit behind the scenes in an organization can be seen through the choice focus. These 'back stage' choices are ones that management tries to influence but knows it cannot fully control. Organizational culture exerts many demands on an executive's life, sometimes in a contradictory way. Indeed culture can be defined by its choices and dilemmas, some of which are endemic to certain industries and professions, as management theorist Charles Hampden-Turner (1994) has shown. Understanding, identifying and working with these organizational realities is an important ingredient of effective coaching.

To complete this theme, it's worth reflecting on the choices that face the largest organization on this planet: human society as a whole. In the coming years, we will make decisions on such issues as climate change, population growth, social equality, ageing and the extraordinary advances of science that are revolutionizing the boundaries of the biological. Choices like this will go a long way towards defining what it means to be human and perhaps even determine our very survival as a species. They will be made in many different ways by citizens and their elected representatives, and by executives in every type of organization – commercial and public, academic and voluntary, governmental and intergovernmental. The importance of creating expertise around making and implementing the right choices could not be greater.

The goals of interactional coaching

This brings us to the goals of interactional coaching, the first of which is to help the coachee make the best possible choices in her situation and to put them into practice, so enabling her to achieve what she wants at work. This is the method's immediate, pragmatic project.

A second, more developmental goal is to help the coachee acquire consciousness of how she makes choices, what motivates her choice-making and how she can improve it. This is called optative awareness, a phrase that draws on the double meaning of the Latin verb, *optare*, 'to choose' and 'to wish'. Optative awareness amounts to a kind of life expertise. Those who possess it know how to assess their situations, identify what they and others want and make optimal choices around their goals and put them into practice. This doesn't mean that their practical and strategic choices always turn out to be the right ones, because nothing can guarantee this. But being able to make and implement choices in an informed way, in the right spirit and using all the resources that are available, is probably as close as we can get to mastering the art of choice.

Implicit in this choice-consciousness is the model's third goal: to develop the client's leadership ability. Leadership is choice-making at its most profound. I don't mean this simply in terms of leading teams or projects or organizations, although a fair amount of interactional coaching's work focuses on this. I mean developing leadership at every level in the workplace. At its core, real leadership is personal leadership: the ability to make the most of your own life, at work and outside it, by making optimal choices about yourself, your values, your relationships and your situation. In this sense, we are all potentially leaders, all the time.

Interactional coaching and other coaching models

The goals of interactional coaching are one way in which it differentiates itself from other models of executive coaching, but there are several others. I have already alluded to its integrated structure. In part, I mean by this that it is a theoretically wide-ranging model, drawing on a unique mix of philosophy, management and leadership studies, organizational behaviour, communication studies and several branches of psychology. At the same time it is very practically-orientated, offering development in communication and interpersonal skills, for example, unlike many coaching models. It is also a form of business coaching with a real commitment to the goals of businesses and the realities of organizational life, but combines this with a deep immersion in psychotherapy and cognitive, social and personality psychology.

Interactional coaching also differentiates itself from other coaching models through its central theoretical principle of human beings as choice-makers in interaction. If to be is to choose oneself, then knowing a person is to understand the unique choices they are making and how they are making them. The content of a person's choices and how they interpret the meaning of their situation cannot be known in advance. So interactional coaching initially focuses on understanding the dynamics of a situation and exploring what it is a client wants, before trying to find the best way to achieve it.

This approach contrasts with several of the leading psychological coaching models, which, in theoretical terms at least, tend to define the person in advance. For example, person-centred and positive psychology models see the person as inherently positive and altruistic and 'motivated by socially constructive directional forces' (Linley and Harrington, 2009: 47). While this may be an admirable presupposition, it does not necessarily help the client to define what is uniquely positive and negative in his situation. Similarly, cognitive-behavioural models introduce a potential theoretical bias into the encounter with the client from the very start, with the notion of universal types of 'irrational' thinking. The concept of 'cognitive distortions' or 'thinking traps' (Neenan, 2006) may be helpful at times but what is irrational in one context may be eminently rational in another. The same criticism may be made of psychodynamic models, with their emphasis on the invariable developmental significance of early family life and the existence of a deep unconscious that disguises the reality of our desires (Orenstein, 2007). These constructs may provide insights but only on the basis of answers about what it is to be human, which have been assumed before any question has actually been asked of the client. For interactional coaching, by contrast, the question of what the client really wants is a mystery that can be revealed only by the coaching process.

If the interactional model is critical of other models' theoretical formulations, this is not to say that it is necessarily critical of their practice, which I suspect may often differ from their theory. This kind of theoretical engagement – which is all too often absent from coaching literature – is made in a wholly constructive spirit. It is based on the idea of creative synthesis (Hegel, 1931), which attempts to take the best from various constructs and give them a new, more consistent theoretical grounding. Coaching has generated many different models – for example, one survey (Whybrow and Palmer, 2006) identifies 28 types of coaching psychology alone – as well as countless tools, techniques and methods. This rich diversity has great advantages but there is a downside in that it is increasingly difficult to define what coaching is and what it does, which is a potential problem for practitioners and users of coaching alike. In many ways resembling existantional coaching (Spinelli and Horner, 2009), interactional coaching attempts to integrate existential philosophy with the many academic disciplines that inform it around the single concept of choice in interaction. This focus carries through to every aspect of its practice, including its primary techniques, tools and principles, as we'll see in Chapter 3. Perhaps by unifying theory and practice the model can offer something useful, not only to its clients but also to the profession of coaching.

Finally, it is important to point out that interactional coaching has been developed for use in a work context and is not a form of psychotherapy. In my experience, the psychological robustness and choice-making ability of executives is generally greater than that of psychotherapy clients and so requires and justifies a different approach. However, it is important that the interactional coach has the psychological expertise to recognize if a coachee's anxiety, depression or other psychological symptoms make him unsuitable for workplace coaching, in order to make a referral to a psychotherapist.

Before going on to explain other aspects of this model, let's now return to the story of Julia, the first of the clients introduced at the beginning of the chapter, to see how interactional coaching works in practice.

2

Development and performance coaching: The case of Julia T.

Development and performance coaching are two of the best known coaching purposes. Development coaching is often described as an assignment without a specific agenda, aimed at the longer-term development of the client. The coachee may be a high potential performer or rising star, whom the organization is keen to nurture and retain. Often the goals of this application of coaching are to develop sustainable abilities and skills that will profit the coachee throughout his career. Performance coaching, by contrast, tends to be triggered by specific problems. These usually relate to perceived shortcomings in an executive's work, perhaps as a result of a poor annual performance review. In some cases, the reason for the coaching may be more urgent, such as an incident in the workplace or the revelation of previously unknown aspects of an employee's behaviour that his line manager or human resources partner feels need to be instantly addressed. The consequences for the client in this kind of situation can be anything from poor performance ratings to outright dismissal or even possible career termination, in which case coaching may represent the client's last chance.

In practice, when a coaching project begins, other issues may emerge, which may blur the distinction between the two purposes. Development coaching can throw up choices around performance, and performance coaching may evolve into a development process. This latter course was followed in the assignment concerning Julia T., a case that, therefore, is well placed to illustrate both performance and development coaching and the practical processes of interactional coaching in general.

The case of Julia T.[*]

'I'm all over the place. I'm in a real mess. I'm going to prove to be a hopeless case, I think.' Julia T., a risk manager in an international bank based in London, tried to hold back her tears as she unfolded her story. It was the first few minutes of our first coaching session. Below the high tower in Canary Wharf in which we sat, I caught a glimpse of the Thames winding towards central London in the haze of a sunny spring morning. 'I used to know exactly where I was going in my career,' she said, looking panicky. 'Now I just seem to stagger from day to day. I don't know what I want.'

Julia had a lot to let out. She was unhappy about many things in her work and her life. She had recently completed a very painful divorce. 'Difficult?,' she said, 'well, he had an affair with one of my friends, what do *you* think? He managed to get the flat as well. He's a lawyer . . .' At the same time as her marriage was breaking up, her 'dream job' in Rome disappeared overnight in a corporate restructuring. 'I just quit,' she said, 'I couldn't be bothered looking for anything else in the bank. I was completely down.'

She had returned to London in a distraught state, moving from one friend's sofa to another, as she put it, and had only just found her own flat. She had been in her current job for four months and was now under 'intense pressure' from her manager to perform at the level her experience and salary merited.

At first, all I could do was listen and try to immerse myself in her situation. After some time, there was a pause and I asked her, 'what do you want to achieve?' She looked slightly shocked by the question:

---

[*] Please note that all the case studies in this book are based on real-life cases. These have been edited, with names changed to preserve the anonymity of the coachees and the client organizations, and in certain cases composite elements have been introduced for illustrative purposes.

> I don't know really. I don't even know if I want to be in banking any more. Maybe I should be doing something else, charity work. Can banks keep growing at the rate they are? This whole growth mania makes me sick at times.

She continued in this vein, questioning whether she wanted to work at all. Bombarded by so many possibilities, she seemed unable to make sense of any of them. 'Can you say what you most do *not* want to be?', I asked her. 'Being this lone subject-matter expert isn't me.' She paused again and then said quietly: 'I guess what I really want is to be involved with people more. And I want to get my career back. I used to be going somewhere, now I don't know.' There was another pause. 'I don't want these feelings all the time. That's for sure.' When I asked her what she meant by 'getting her career back', she replied: 'I want to have a clear direction. I want to get some respect from the people here.'

For a brief moment she looked more positive. It was as though she was starting to think about making choices again. Life seemed to have stripped her of choices recently: her ex-husband and her bank had presented her with a fait accompli. Even her current job had been something of an accident. She had only taken it because a loyal friend had set up the job interview. All the choosing recently had been done for her. For a few seconds she articulated something that was a glimpse of a possible future but Julia was still very tied up in the past.

Her previous job seemed to have been a golden age for Julia. She had loved working in Rome. She was fluent in Italian, happy in her marriage and had, as she described it, 'the best boss in the world'. Maria was charismatic, warm and generous. 'If you were on her side she was completely on yours, which was fantastic. I got so much out of her in terms of confidence and sheer joie de vivre.' She contrasted Maria to her current boss, Jonathan, references to whom wove in and out of Julia's conversation. The comparison was unfavourable to Jonathan, to put it mildly. 'He's cold, scheming, mediocre. He just does what the rule book tells him to do. Can't relate to people at all.'

This wasn't my impression of Jonathan, I had to admit, having met him in my coaching briefing, along with the bank's human resources director. Yes, Jonathan had a rather deadpan, unemotional manner but he seemed fair and genuinely concerned about Julia. However, I tried to put this thought aside, to 'bracket' it as a possible hypothesis, and returned to being as open as I could be to what Julia was saying.

When we came to discuss Julia's interactional map, Jonathan figured very prominently. Julia had little to do with Jonathan's boss and had found it hard to establish good working relationships with her peers in Jonathan's team. There had been several run-ins over procedure, where she had been critical of their risk management and generally dismissive of the bank's old-fashioned ways. 'They're different,' she said, 'they're people who've been here all their careers – they don't know what life is like outside. I'm seen as some sort of alien or newcomer to the village who'll take twenty years to get accepted.'

'How important is it that you establish a good relationship with your colleagues?', I asked. She said nothing and gave me a rather sullen look, with a half shrug of her shoulders. I went on, 'to what extent are they your colleagues and to what extent your clients?' 'I suppose,' she sighed, 'they are in effect my internal customers. I probably do need to do something there.'

Julia also had junior colleagues who did not formally report to her but who worked for her on different projects. She got on well with these executives, who seemed to respect her knowledge and her concern for their development. Talking about them, she became more animated and even laughed at herself, picturing their bewilderment at her changes of policy in one particular project.

Coach: What could make things better with these colleagues?

Coachee: Well, I guess they should be reporting to me. That way I wouldn't have all these misunderstanding with Jonathan and my peers. That way I wouldn't be changing my mind all the time. I never used to do that.

Coach: Who would be able to change their reporting line?
Coachee: It's up to Jonathan, I suppose.

All roads seemed to lead back to Jonathan and yet Julia was very resistant to the idea that her boss was really influential. She went into another attack on him: his coldness, his bureaucratic manner, his mechanical efficiency. In a real sense, I felt she had difficulty seeing him as a person at all. Shortly after this, we ended our session, but this was one of the strongest impressions I took out of it.

By the second session, 10 days later, Julia's attitude seemed to have changed. She was more focused and less tearful, if still fairly subdued. 'I think I want to make a go of it here,' she said. 'Whatever banking is or isn't, it's what I know, and I probably need to stick with it.' She also seemed clearer about the importance of interacting with Jonathan more successfully. 'Like it or not, I guess I've got to change something with him.'

This was an important development and a confirmation for me that Julia's situation was appropriate for coaching rather than psychotherapy, which had seemed a possibility at the start. It pointed us in the direction of a coaching action plan, but first I wanted to get to know more about Julia's personality.

'I'm a very emotional person, you might have guessed that', she said smiling wistfully. 'My feelings drive me on – though I can be really logical when I have to be.' As an expert on some of the most complex transactions that the bank undertook, Julia had a very sharp, analytical mind but she felt that this was often undermined by her emotional states. 'I get very stressed these days – I used to be carefree but now I just panic about everything.' It seemed that she found it difficult to really analyse her feelings or what caused her stress.

She described herself as an extravert. 'I love people,' she said, 'but my life seems very lonely at the moment.' She saw herself as a supportive person. She liked helping others and being part of a team. She had always worked in a support function. 'But I've never had a problem getting on with people in the front office', she said, referring to the trading and sales departments. 'I can be feisty, if I have to be. Too feisty sometimes!' She saw herself as an accommodator rather than an innovator. She realized it was strange that her colleagues took her for someone who wanted to change everything. 'I don't rock the boat for the sake of it. It's just I've worked at other places that seem to have better ways of doing things.'

What about her self-confidence? 'Shot to pieces', she said dramatically. 'It was always a bit precarious but I think I used to feel fairly certain about what I could accomplish. Now I worry about everything. I sometimes think did I really do that in my previous jobs? Was that *me*?' Later she added, 'some days I feel like an intruder here, as if I'd stolen someone else's security card'.

The coaching action plan that emerged from our discussions was simple and direct, appropriate for the 10 sessions we still had ahead of us. The plan had four main objectives:

- Improve Julia's interactions with Jonathan.
- Develop the possibility of a managerial role for Julia.
- Build more productive relationships with her colleagues.
- Work on her self-confidence and stress management.

Of these objectives, we agreed that her interaction with Jonathan was probably the most urgent. 'What does he think of your work?', I asked. 'Not much', she said rather bitterly. 'He doesn't think I do much for a start.' When we tried to ascertain why this was, Julia said:

> The truth is, he doesn't see a fraction of what I do on projects – or how long it takes me to sort out certain problems. He's in his office all the time or in meetings, endless meetings. I'm used to bosses who are out on the floor, making their presence felt.

'Do you tell him what you're doing?', I enquired. 'Well, he should know – that's his job', was Julia's initial response but, after further reflection, she agreed that she didn't communicate well what she was actually doing. She took his enquiries into what she was working on as implicit criticisms of her and tended to either shut down completely or change the subject, often by complaining about something. I suggested to her that in the end she seemed to confirm his view that she was not doing very much. She looked equivocal at this and gazed out of the window.

She seemed to be in a kind of half-way house. On the one hand, she'd begun to realize that Jonathan could be the key to her future development; on the other hand, she didn't seem to be prepared to do anything that could be interpreted as trying to please him. In the end, she came up with the solution to this dilemma herself. 'I need to show him what I'm doing, to show him how wrong he is about me', she said, with a look of defiance I hadn't seen in her before.

We spent some time going over what she would say, trying to find the appropriate tone for her: assertive but not aggressive. She seemed to hit the right notes fairly quickly.

'How well do you think you listen to him?', I then asked her, because at times I had the sense that Julia was not listening to me very attentively. She would hold eye contact very well but I had the sense that she was attending only to her own thoughts. Sometimes her responses seemed subtly unconnected to what I had been talking about.

'He's hard to listen to, to be honest, he's got this rather whispery voice that is very monotonous and he just goes on and on at times. . . . I don't know, we often seem to be at cross-purposes.' I suggested that she make an effort to listen him, even paraphrase what he was asking her, so as to be absolutely sure that she had understood what he was saying. We tried a brief experiment in this and Julia found it harder than she thought to repeat what I had said. 'OK, I'll give it a try with him', she said a shade reluctantly.

The meeting with Jonathan, as Julia revealed in the next session, turned out to be a success. Julia had persuasively outlined the work she had been undertaking. Jonathan had been impressed and had apologized for underestimating her workload, an apology that had gone down particularly well with Julia. She, in her turn, had tried much harder to listen to him and had begun to appreciate some of the subtleties of what he was saying and even to pick up a sense of his concern for her. She said she wanted to impress him further – a sign to me that she was moving beyond her ambivalence towards him and making a clear, positive choice.

'He's Mr Meticulous, whereas I'm all over the shop. I need to try and get my act together – or at least give that impression', Julia added with a quick laugh. We looked at the rather random way in which she organized her day. She realized her chaotically ordered desk probably gave him – and others – a rather poor impression. Relatively trivial as this may have seemed, keeping it tidy looked like a comparatively easy way of impressing Jonathan, so Julia opted for this quick win.

With the relationship fast improving and a real mutual respect growing, Julia moved on to her next objective: managing a team. We discussed her strategy in proposing this to Jonathan, trying to anticipate how he might react – and how Julia might respond to his reaction. This was probably time well spent because, in the event, Jonathan was initially unenthusiastic about Julia's suggestion. But Julia didn't take his response as a rejection of her proposal, suspecting that his customary cautiousness lay behind his reticence. She repeated her suggestion a few weeks later and this time he agreed to it. Julia would take over responsibility for two employees during a probationary period. Her mood was ebullient as she related this to me.

She wanted to talk through the specifics of managing a team, having been 'out of practice' for a while, but it was soon clear that she had some very good ideas about managing in general and some specific insights into her new direct reports. Perhaps the main thing she had to watch out for, she concluded, was being too indulgent. 'I've got to be assertive when I need to be and not let my emotions cloud my judgment but', she added meaningfully, 'I'm starting to get a much better grip of my feelings.'

This was evident in the way she now dealt with setbacks, because her path was not a straight one and there were several reversals and blockages along the way. It seemed her whole way of choosing how to act was changing. For instance, one day she said she snapped at Jonathan, when he made a remark that she felt betrayed ignorance of his subject. She stormed away from him, with a hollow feeling that she was caught in a trap from which she could never escape. Yet an hour later, she was able to put her head around Jonathan's office door and apologize for her outburst. He accepted her apology with 'typically understated good grace', she said. This remark suddenly put me in mind of her former boss, Maria, and I wondered how she would have reacted to this kind of criticism. 'Oh you wouldn't have wanted to cross her. She'd be like a viper. Jonathan doesn't take offence like that.' I was struck by the very different picture of the two managers that seemed to be emerging.

Julia's self-confidence grew significantly through her improved interactions with others but it was also important to look at her interactions with herself. Her self-dialogue still seemed to be dominated by negative images and thoughts. One source of these was her secondary school, an extremely prestigious academic establishment, which appeared to have left her with feelings of great inadequacy.

Coachee: I thought I was bright until I went there. I *am* intelligent but compared to most of the girls there I was a dunce. It was the kind of place where if you don't end up in the Cabinet or with a career in Hollywood they think you're a complete failure.

Coach: They do or you do?

Coachee: Me, I suppose. I just seem to set higher standards for myself than I can ever attain.

Coach: What does that do for you?

Coachee: I don't know. I guess I always know where I am.

Coach: Maybe it stops you listening to yourself and where you really are.

We tried to analyse this process, which often led to Julia feeling overwhelmed by self-criticism. 'It's my fear of ending up with nothing, I guess', she said. 'In my imagination, I go from one mistake to another until I am finished, just done; over as a person.' 'So you're looking into the future', I said, 'and deciding that it's got nothing for you?' 'Something like that', she replied.

From the interactional coach's point of view, it might be easy at this juncture to point out that the future does not yet exist. We construct it. We attempt to define it but it remains unknowable. We create an interpretation of ourselves and then project it forwards and, in Julia's case, become depressed at what rebounds back, as though the future was creating us rather than our creating it. I tried to emphasize to Julia that she had a choice about her attitude to the future.

Coachee: Does that mean I can always be positive?
Coach: Not always.
Coachee: Does that mean I will never again be negative?
Coach: Probably not.
Coachee: What does it mean then?
Coach: That you can always make a difference to your mood. How much of a difference is up to you.
Coachee: You know, perhaps negativity stops me from getting above myself. After all, if you hope for too much, you get disappointed.
Coach: So are you deliberately disappointing yourself in advance?
Coachee: It seems like I'm doing it rather too well!

By the time we arrived at our last couple of sessions, there was a distinct change in the nature of the coaching. Julia was now very much making her own choices and reporting them to me. Sometimes we would look at these choices and see if the opposite of what she had chosen revealed anything interesting, or examine practical ways of implementing other choices. Julia was clearly beginning to thrive as a manager and was about to take on an enlarged team. She was also starting to develop effective, and in some cases very warm, working relationships with her colleagues. She also reflected regularly on what was going on for her emotionally and intellectually. Throughout our early sessions the shadow of her failed marriage seemed never far away, but by our final sessions she seemed to have come to terms with it. She said that she was now seeing someone else and was much happier.

Another interesting sign of her changed attitude to herself was her attitude to her former boss: 'I've been thinking a lot about Maria recently', she said. 'She really didn't support me at all, when our department was closed down. She looked after herself but I was left with a lot of warm words but no deeds.' The contrast between the two bosses seemed to have come full circle. Jonathan, with his unassuming, dry manner, seemed to be genuinely concerned to help others while Maria, for all her warmth and charisma, apparently had been much more manipulative.

Put in terms of her interactional style preferences, Julia now saw herself as more dominant but less aggressive. She was more self-confident, more able to focus on the best of her emotions rather than the worst and more capable of being innovative in areas in which she felt comfortable. Her interactional skills had also developed considerably, enabling her to use her technical ability to support others rather than intimidate them. It was no accident that the word 'leadership' started to crop up in our conversations, mainly from the feedback Julia was getting from her colleagues. Anyone who can go through the chaos of wrong choices and bad luck and come out of it, knowing how to make the right choices, is likely to have developed some genuine leadership skills.

The change was also evident in Julia's attitude to time – her addiction to a golden but, as it turned out, rather illusory past had given way to a stronger, more clear-sighted hold on the future. This showed in the way she organized everyday work – although her desk by all accounts was still fairly chaotic – and in her restored sense of having a career ahead of her. 'I definitely want to stay here for another five years or so. After that, who knows? I certainly wouldn't mind taking on a senior role eventually – perhaps even Jonathan's job', she laughed.

'The main thing is that I know myself better', she said shortly before we concluded our final session. She went on to say:

> And that makes it much easier to get on with others. I don't think I'll get fooled by others so easily again. And maybe I won't be so foolish myself either, because I think I was probably quite a pain when you and I first met.

I smiled but said nothing. We'd started our sessions in the late spring and by now it was the dead of winter, with the odd snowflake drifting in the air above Canary Wharf. But there was nothing cold about Julia's presence. She had once seemed defeated by events but she now exuded the energy of someone fully engaged with her life. She was surer of herself, surer of what she wanted in her work and much more able to achieve it. That seemed like a good enough place to end our work together.

3

The practice of interactional coaching: Techniques, tools and principles

Julia T.'s story unfolded apparently seamlessly but behind the scenes, as it were, there are techniques, principles and methods at work that guide the interactional approach. Before going on to other coaching purposes and case studies, it is important to examine how concepts such as the interactional self and the choice cycle inform what the interactional coach does at a practical level.

Good practice and good theory go together. A coaching model is, in part, a collection of techniques and methods and its appeal will be evaluated in terms of how useful these are in helping clients to achieve their objectives. But a model is also a theoretical construct, a high-level description of a practice, which implies a particular set of attitudes to, and assumptions about, the world. In this context, it will be judged by its internal theoretical coherence and consistency, both increasingly important issues for potential users of coaching as they try to choose between the many different models on offer.

Coaching is a particular form of dialogue and all human dialogue can be said to consist of three elements: listening, questioning and stating. In this chapter, we look at the methodology of interactional coaching through these three elements, focusing on the key questions the coach asks in the diagnostic stage of coaching and the process of choice that underpins the 'expert listening' that coaching requires. We also say something about the philosophical principles of interactional coaching, the technique of oppositional enquiry and the interactional approach to personality analysis. The chapter concludes by examining practical skills development and the nature of the coaching relationship.

Questioning

Questioning is a central activity in coaching and in truth-gathering in general. As the philosopher Hans-Georg Gadamer (1975: 328) observed, 'the priority of the question over the answer . . . is the basis of the concept of knowledge'. Asking the right question is often the key to finding the right answer.

Usually the first questions that occur in a coaching assignment arise during the pre-coaching phase, the all-important conversations that the coach usually has with the sponsor of the coaching, the client's line manager, coaching director or human resources professional, or the client herself. These questions, spoken and unspoken, are often choices. Is the organization committed to coaching? How many sessions are available? The coach may be wondering if the client has a good sense of what he wants or where he wants to go, in which case the assignment can focus on how to practically get there. Or, at this very early stage, does it seem that the coaching is first and foremost about helping the client decide where he wants to go? Of course, any of the specific purposes of coaching that we are exploring in this book may also emerge at this point.

When it comes to the first session with the client, the choice focus is likely to continue with questions related to the client's life and career narratives. Typically, these questions will include the following:

- What choices led you here? (This is an opportunity to explore the key choices the client has made in his life, education and career, focusing on the key turning points and 'cross-roads moments' that have shaped him.)
- What choices are you now making? (This brings out the client's goals, aims and purposes at work.)
- What choices are you not making? (This can help to identify the challenges, concerns or dilemmas that the client is wrestling with or has not yet come to terms with.)

- What choices could you be making? (This may open up the conversation to a wider, more imaginative look at the possible courses of action the client could take.)
- What choices are you making but don't realize it? (This is often a very telling question that prompts the client to identify assumptions or prejudgments she had not been fully aware of or positive appreciations that she has taken for granted.)

The cardinal questions

Another set of important questions for the interactional coach are the so-called cardinal questions. These questions represent the three dimensions of the interactional self (time, self and others) and are particularly effective in helping to identify what the client wants and how he can achieve it, as we saw in Julia's story.

The first cardinal question is: What do you want to achieve? It is a question that takes us to the heart of the matter, the desires that motivate our choices. This is in part because it puts us firmly into the time dimension of the self, pitching us forward on that track to the future that we are always following, even though we may not be aware of it.

The second question of this type is: Who are you – or how would you describe yourself? This takes us to the central dimension of the self. It addresses the professional compe-tences the coachee possesses or needs to develop to achieve his project and how his personal values relate to it. It also raises the question of how well the client knows himself. This type of enquiry quickly builds up a picture of what the client has going for and against him, in terms of bringing his ambitions to fruition.

The third cardinal question is: Who do you need to interact with to achieve this – and how do you need to interact with them? This takes us to the 'others' dimension of the self, immediately alerting us to the social context in which work takes place. The client's interactional map, which we'll return to in detail in Chapter 7, reveals her most significant relationships in her work context. Exploring this web of influence tells us who she needs to interact with in order to achieve what she wants and indicates the interactional skills she needs in order to do so.

Listening

Listening is so fundamental to coaching that the practice could well be called a form of expert listening. And by listening, I mean not only silent, auditory attention to the client but, in its widest sense, an observational activity facilitated by questions, probing, enquiry or interpretation aimed at clarifying the real meaning of what the client is saying.

Expert listening in coaching can be sharply contrasted with the listening that often occurs in ordinary conversation, whether in social life or the workplace. Everyday listening can be superficial. We may listen to what our co-conversationalist is saying only to the point where his words trigger thoughts of our own. Our own desire to articulate our own experiences or point of view may limit our ability to hear what is really being said. The priorities of everyday conversation of this kind can be described as stating, questioning and listening (SQL). Stating (i.e. forms of talking) tends to be the predominant activity, so much so that many conversations can be described as the swapping of statements, in the form of opinions, feelings, experiences or stories.

The coaching conversation is different. It reverses the priorities of ordinary conversation (i.e. SQL) and creates a coachee-focused dialogue, based on listening, questioning and stating (LQS). The coachee will still make more statements than listen; indeed the coach may encourage him to make more statements than usual. But for the coach, listening becomes a crucial activity, with questioning and stating often supporting the listening process.

In practice, I would suggest that all coaching approaches rely on the power of listening, but trying to define listening theoretically may be more difficult for many models. From an interactional standpoint, the definition couldn't be clearer because it takes us back to the model's theoretical core. Listening in everyday practice represents the existentialist idea that 'existence is prior to essence' (Sartre, 1948: 29). This refers to the attempt to understand the world by observing what is really before us rather than imposing a pre-selected framework or 'essence' onto it. Indeed, existential theory could be called a philosophy of listening. It says that in order to understand reality we must listen to it, observe it, feel it and try to open ourselves to this reality, so that it can speak out, as it were. And this won't be easy because we are constantly intentionally connected with that reality, caught between the meaning it sends us and the meaning we impose on it.

Interactionally, there are three types of expert listening that correspond to the three stages of the choice cycle: open listening focuses on the possibilizing, identification stage of choice; evidential listening is more closely associated with the probabilizing, selection phase; and conclusive listening embodies the actualizing, implementation stage of the choice cycle.

Open listening (possibilizing)

The goal of open listening is to open up to what the client is really saying. It is essentially a form of choice management and is often the most difficult aspect of expert listening to master because it seems to go against the flow of the choice cycle. One of the human brain's greatest assets is its ability to quickly size up situations and opt for appropriate actions. We can move at lightning speed from initial impressions to conclusions. The problem is that our conclusions are often wrong and, the more complex the situation, the more likely this is to be true. Open listening means pushing against the flow of our thoughts and resisting too rapid a movement downstream. It is essentially a process of deferring choices, suspending the interpretative process that leads from a possibility to a conclusion, in order to identify as many possibilities as are available.

For the coach, open listening means coping with one of the biggest threats to understanding the client's situation: our human need to shape meaning and to come up with solutions to problems. The vivid impressions thrown up by a client, particularly if he is in a state of distress, may seem to demand definite responses rather than openness. The coach may have to remain in a state of uncertainty for longer than might seem pleasant, suspending choice for a good while before he can contemplate clear lines of action or any reassurances about how the coaching project will proceed.

The challenge is even greater for many executives. Over many years of running coaching skills workshops, I have found that open listening is one of the hardest skills for managers to acquire, especially those who think of themselves as professional problem-solvers. Not being able to sort out a problem may make some executives feel inadequate. The statement, 'I don't know yet', even if unspoken, can seem like a defeat. For such a person, any response may be better than none, with the consequence that the real problem with which she is grappling is often not detected.

One effective technique for controlling a listener's movement through the choice cycle is called 'bracketing'. This is based on Husserl's (1931) phenomenological method, which attempts to describe reality as it is, in part by identifying the mental prejudgments that we bring to any situation (Spinelli, 1989). For example, the client may say: 'I'm no longer that concerned about promotion.' The coach's instantaneous private response to this may be, 'this is about avoiding having a difficult conversation with your boss'. But instead of finalizing this choice, the coach mentally puts it to one side, treating it as a hypothesis that may be revisited later. There may be other reasons why the coachee said what he said and these need to be given a chance to emerge. We might say that open listening is about exploring, not commuting. It involves being prepared to head out into the unknown rather than travelling from A to B. This is not always easy but it can be extremely rewarding, once achieved.

Evidential listening (probabilizing)

What substantiates this statement? How does this assertion connect with that? This kind of self-enquiry on the part of the coach indicates a second stage of listening, which is concerned with evidence. Possibility starts to give way to probability. The client's choices may seem concrete but this solidity can be misleading, just as seemingly robust clouds are revealed to be no more than vapour when an aeroplane flies through them. A coachee may state that she is not liked by her team but the coach will want to ascertain if this assumption is based on real evidence rather than hearsay, speculation or the coachee's own feelings about herself. In this phase, open listening gives way to a more dogged form of attention, creating a zig-zagging dialectic between open and closed attitudes.

Expert listening is not only a question of the spoken word: it also extends to observation. Paying attention to a client's non-verbal communication – whether it's his tone of voice or facial expression, the movement of a hand or the shifting of a posture – may indicate to the coach other levels of possibility and probability. It might be that the client makes a positive statement – such as 'I'm really looking forward to developing a new customer base' – and yet the tremor in his voice or his clenched fist suggests a more complex, mixed attitude.

Conclusive listening (actualizing)

The third phase of listening is about moving the choice process towards action. Often the effect of open listening is enough to help the client see his way forward, perhaps for the first time. And yet, for all our love of conclusions, sometimes the process stalls. The client's conversation may circle around, weaving in and out of possibilities but never settling on a conclusion. In such cases, the coach may ask the kind of questions that move the client downstream to consider probabilities or even skip straight to possible actions. For example, the coach may say: 'So you think this could mean a change of role for you?' or 'Are you saying you think you have to cancel this order?'. Focusing on cause and effect can also be useful, as in: 'What effect will this have on your team?' or 'How do you think this behaviour will impact your boss?'

For the coach, trying to model effective choosing through expert listening is part of his or her overall remit to help the client achieve what he wants. And for many clients, it is the most striking aspect of coaching. One extremely loquacious sales manager once said to me: 'I've got to do more of the main thing I've noticed that you do: listen.' Or, as Heidegger (1962: 208) once observed: 'To keep silent does not mean to be dumb.'

Oppositional enquiry

What else is the interactional coach listening out for? In many cases, it is the interactional forces at play in the client's situation, by which I mean the polarities, conflicts and oppositions that impinge most on her. These oppositions may stem from her own values, beliefs and assumptions or from the kind of competitive relationships that abound in the working environment or from the interaction between the two. Either way, where there are opposites there are energy and meaning, which may act as levers of change in coaching.

Identifying the client's oppositional values often involves clarifying the direction of their interaction. Some values are horizontal, vying for supremacy in any situation; others are more vertical, ranked in a hierarchy of meaning, where one is always valued more highly than the other. So one client may see the opposition 'working life–private life' horizontally, each having value depending on the context. Another client may experience this interaction vertically, with her work being seen an intrinsically superior to her private life. By identifying these value dynamics, we can help to delineate the key parameters of the client's world.

Oppositional enquiry is a flexible approach that can work with most statements the client makes. In one form, it may be simply a matter of the coach taking a phrase or remark and asking the client what is its opposite, like flipping over a coin. We might envisage this process as looking at a conversational subject as though it were a three-dimensional object, which we examine from every angle, front and back, top and bottom. So a client may say 'fairness is important to me'. When the coach asks how he defines 'unfair' one client may say, 'it's unfair that talent is not recognized', whereas another client may say, 'it's unfair that people get paid more than others for the same job'. In this way, a coachee's unique worldview may emerge.

Identifying positive and negative polarities is another elucidatory form of oppositional enquiry. Questions that illuminate the positive/negative field of interaction include:

- Who do you most admire in the company and who do you least admire?
- What is best about the company and what is worst?
- What gives you most satisfaction at work and what stresses you most?

Focusing on a client's positive and negative interpretation of himself can also be useful. It may highlight a side of himself that he does not recognize as positive. For example, clients intent on high achievement are often prone to excessive self-criticism, which can reduce their ability to make the choices that are best for them. In such cases, the coach may see an opportunity to offer positive feedback or engage in other forms of confidence-building. At the same time, the coach may also need to focus on the negative aspects of coachees' situations, especially where they tend to disregard their professional shortcomings or underestimate their lack of resources. This kind of bias can be equally distorting when it comes to realistically evaluating their options at work.

In working with these opposites, interactional practice has something in common with coaching approaches that favour the positive aspects of human reality, as well as models more inclined to emphasize the negative aspects. The difference is that for the interactional model both dimensions are vital and cannot be understood in isolation from one another, which is why identifying the positive and negative dynamics that actually exist within the client's world, without a prior theoretical agenda, is so important.

Reinterpretation: Changing the choice landscape

Oppositional enquiry often helps the client to create different interpretations of the world. By pointing out oppositions, the coach may be helping the client to change her 'choice landscape' by effectively offering her alternatives to the choices she is already making. This might involve a shift between the self dimension and the dimension of others. For example, a client may be so convinced that others are to blame for the failure of an initiative that he is unable to see that he himself has a responsibility for it. If the coach says, 'I am trying to figure out where *you* are in this relationship', this can introduce the much-needed dimension of others into a very one-sided interpretation of the situation. The function of oppositional enquiry here, as elsewhere, is to turn around the conversational theme, so to speak, and in so doing break the hold that a particular angle of perception can have over coachee and coach alike.

Often known as 'reframing' in psychotherapy (e.g. Satir, 1967), reinterpretation is a core element of most coaching practices, although its theoretical implications are often not recognized. Reframing is possible because we live in a world of interactional richness, where at any moment a choice of meanings is available to us. If meaning was fixed, this kind of reinterpretation would be much more difficult to achieve. It is because we live in time, in a state of change, choosing and re-choosing our interpretations of ourselves and others, that we can reinterpret our world relatively easily. In this way, the interactional model links this basic coaching practice to its core theory rather than seeing it simply as a technique that 'works'.

Oppositional logic

Underlying oppositional enquiry – and indeed the whole interactional approach – is a way of thinking that we can call interactional or oppositional logic. This draws on the tradition of dialectical thinking within existential and phenomenological theory. Originally developed by Hegel (1931), the dialectic is the idea that interaction is at the heart of human existence and that change is a new reality, or synthesis, that emerges from the interaction of opposites. Oppositional logic is not so much a formal system as a way of making sense of the world.

Here are six propositions that capture something of this way of thinking:

1 Meaning can only be understood in a situation. 'A rose is a rose is a rose', it was once said (Stein, 1922), but a rose in a horticultural catalogue is quite different from a rose in a lover's hand. At any point in time all situations are connected, so potentially the totality of these situations is relevant to the meaning of any element of it.

2 Change is constant because we live in time, which is a continual unfolding of the new. Life is not a series of fixed points but a process of becoming. Arrive at your destination and you have already started another journey.

3 Reality is oppositional, which means that contradictions are not necessarily mutually exclusive as conventional logic's law of non-contradiction suggests. We can only understand entity A by understanding entity B, rather than eliminating or rejecting it as false. For example, we can only understand darkness by means of our experience of light, and, when we really examine them, perhaps all feelings are 'mixed' feelings.

4 Reality is inherently ambiguous, changing according to the point of observation. There is no absolute position that can be said to be true within a set of interactions, although the more we are aware of these interactions the closer we can get to the best truth available.

5 In any situation, there is a tension or balance between interacting forces. Balance may seem to be a static concept but it is actually highly dynamic. Finding the right balance in any situation – which is by no means necessarily the mid-point – is often the key to making the most of it.

6 Optimal choice is the balance between total freedom and total non-freedom – the recognition of what you can do in a situation and what the situation imposes. This 'best possible' choice may be the most authentic state we can achieve, which is perhaps why Kierkegaard (1996: 81) said that 'to choose oneself' is the same thing as 'to know oneself'.

The role of personality biases: The Interactional Styles Outliner (ISO)

The Interactional Styles Outliner (ISO) is another form of oppositional enquiry, which uses a type of interactional logic to create insights into the client's personality. Any personality assessment, for all the marketing mystique that sometimes surrounds it, is simply a series of questions that offer the client a range of choices, often in hypothetical situations. With enough face-to-face time the coach would probably glean a sense of how the client will respond to these situations, but time is not always available. The ISO can help to accelerate this information-gathering process, as well as offering the client new forms of self-knowledge.

The ISO is not a formal personality theory, although it loosely corresponds to the so-called Big Five personality dimensions that have consistently emerged from exhaustive factor analysis by psychologists over recent years (e.g. Costa and McCrea, 2003). It is essentially a coaching tool that has developed organically from years of practical client work and is designed to help coach and client alike to gain insights into their 'personal dialectics': the particular interactions that dominate in any particular situation. It may be applied quite informally, through the questioning that spontaneously emerges out of the coaching conversation, or through a more formal questionnaire.

The ISO is based around five pairs of interactional style: dominant/supportive, introvert/extravert, rationally-orientated/emotionally-orientated, originating/accommodating and self-confident/self-questioning. These are not normative dimensions by which to judge a client's talents; they are simply a value-neutral description of different styles of personality at work. Identifying the client's personal dialectics in this way gives an indication of the skills he needs to develop in order to move more flexibility across the spectrum. It also often reveals the kind of balance of oppositional values necessary for achievement and helps him see the advantages and disadvantages of his personality biases. In short, it enables him to use his personality style as an asset rather than a constraint when it comes to choice-making.

The first ISO polarity is concerned with power, which is such a telling factor in organizational life. Some executives tend to have a dominant, power-orientated self-image in which they see themselves exercising control over others. Their self-dialogue may focus heavily on winners and losers, on the need for discipline and direction. This bias may seem to offer an advantage in the organizational power stakes but it can have a deleterious effect on the very people whom the executive needs to deliver results. By contrast, supportive professionals are often highly effective in creating solidarity and getting the best out of others. However, their lack of assertiveness and their readiness to go along with others can sometimes result in low personal morale and compliance with inefficiency and poor leadership.

Social orientation also influences an executive's work style. Introverts may have the advantage over extraverts of being focused on their work, good at self-analysis and less liable to waste time in needless socializing but may find it difficult to impress others or network across the organiza-tion. In social situations introverts may experience stress or a high degree of effort in processing interpersonal choices, which may make it more difficult for them to put them into action. Extraverts may be more able to actualize a range of choices and less likely to feel regret afterwards if they don't succeed.

A rational orientation may help executives in that they are likely to enjoy planning and be measured in their behav-iour, but they may lack spontaneity, intuitiveness or sensi-tivity to the feelings of others. On the other hand, executives who are driven by their feelings may be more in touch with their colleagues but need to be more consistent in their behaviour and logical in their action planning.

Origination (readiness to innovate)/accommodation (respect for convention) is another crucial organizational polarity. The ability of originating executives to produce many new solutions to existing problems may give them an advantage over more accommodating executives, who tend be more respectful of the status quo and prefer more tried and tested ways of working. Yet originators often fail to get their ideas accepted because they lack the interactional skills to persuade others and work effectively in group situations.

The fifth interactional style pairing, self-confidence and self-questioning, is another vital factor in executive success. Self-confident executives will tend to predict more success for themselves than those who are diffident about their own ability, and by doing so often increase the chances of making that success a reality. Yet overconfidence can also lead to many a corporate fall. Self-questioning is the ideal antidote to overconfidence but, taken to extremes, it can be vitiating and deprive executives of their ability to perform anywhere near their true level.

Personality assessments can be a source of real insight, which is one of the reasons for their popularity among organizations and clients. From an interactional viewpoint, it is worth stressing that the individual is a mixture of the choosing and the chosen, of freedom and fate. Some of our personal preferences and ways of interacting in adult life have been inherited genetically or socially formed at an early age, according to contemporary psychology (Gleitman et al., 2010). How we re-invent what has been invented for us by factors that are initially outside our control is immensely significant. The more we become aware of our personal dialectics, the more we can control the balance between what we choose and what has been chosen for us.

Stating

One-to-one skills learning

So far we've focused on listening and questioning but the interactional coach is also likely to make statements. These may be based on professional expertise, academic learning or personal experience and will be offered in the spirit of openness, in which rejection is not regarded as criticism. Some of these statements will be around practical skills coaching, which is an option for the interactional approach, as illustrated by the listening and interpersonal skills that helped Julia to build a new relationship with her manager. I believe there are major advantages to be had by offering clients the opportunities to refresh or develop inter-actional or managerial skills. Without these competences, clients may turn down a particular strategy because they fear they lack the resources to implement it or fail in the execution of a perfectly good plan. In either case it is hard to say that the coachee has a fully free choice, which is a powerful incentive for helping him to acquire the appro-priate skills. Ultimately, adult learning is about making choices to adopt certain ways of behaving and reject others. Skills coaching simply facilitates these choices.

Many of the skills necessary for organizational success are interactional in the sense that they require the ability of dialogue with others. And, as we'll see in Chapter 17, many managerial skills, such as setting strategy, delegating or recruiting the right personnel, are fundamentally about managing choices. So, in a real sense, the practical skills are simply an extension of the interactional coaching remit of encouraging choices through increasing interaction with self, others and time, rather than a qualitatively different activity.

The interactional model differentiates itself from many coaching models by its position on skills learning. Although some cognitive-behavioural approaches favour skills coaching, other coaching models prefer a dialogue-only approach. For example, person-centred coaches claim that a 'non-directive' attitude encourages the coachee to take responsibility for her own choices (Joseph and Bryant-Jeffries, 2009). But in my view it is wrong to suggest that refraining from skills learning implies that the coach is not directing the client. After all, a coach can indicate her prefer-ences by a look or a silence more strongly than by any state-ment. In interactional coaching, all types of learning are offered to the client but not imposed on her. Her choice of accepting or declining this offer is itself part of the coaching process. And, of course, the client's most important choice will be whether to implement any skills she has learned in the workplace itself, a choice that takes place outside the coaching room, far away from the presence of the coach.

The coaching relationship

In the end, the most significant interaction in coaching is the relationship between the coach and the coachee, which often overflows generalizations about technique and approach. It is a special human relationship that is unique to each coaching project. In foregrounding the importance of the coaching relationship, the interactional model is in agreement with coaching models as diverse as multidimensional (Orenstein, 2007), business (Shaw and Linnecar, 2007), existential (Spinelli, 2010) and relational (de Haan, 2008).

The coaching relationship has something of an oppositional, even paradoxical, character. For example, the coach is supportive of the client, in that he or she is warmly committed to helping the client's project and yet may have to be very challenging in order to realize that project. As we've seen, the coach may help to reveal many positive aspects of the client's life and work for the first time and yet also expose her to more negative feedback than ever before. Indeed, the coach's ability 'to say the unsayable', especially to senior managers, may be his main asset. The coaching relationship is also an interaction of equals, but equals who are very different in that each comes to the encounter from different angles and with different levels of experience and knowledge. This view, incidentally, is at odds with the traditional scientist-practitioner model (Corrie and Lane, 2009) espoused by some coaching psychology models, which implies the superiority of 'scientific' knowledge over other forms of knowing.

The quality of learning in the coaching relationship is another of its prime features. One of the benefits of coaching that clients most often note is that it creates an environment that enables them to 'step back' from everyday working life. This stepping back involves another opposition, the interaction between normal thinking and a more penetrating form of reflection, which may be called super-reflection. Organizational thinking can be driven by the immediate, the urgent, the conventional. Often quantity can seem to be more important than quality, as the sheer amount of information-processing that needs to be done in a working day limits the clarity and originality of an executive's thinking. At best, super-reflective awareness rises above the day-to-day and at the same time seems to penetrate to a deeper level, so that the thinker is aware not only of the choices he is making but also the whole process of choosing. As such, it is an asset that is far more adaptable and enduring than any one-off solution can ever be.

We'll return to the qualities of the interactional coach in Chapter 21 but one requirement is incontestable: concern for the client. The coach needs to care about the client for the client's own sake. This doesn't mean that the coach can ever be entirely selfless: on the contrary, being conscious of his or her own desires and choices (optative awareness) is the only real way of limiting the negative effects of selfishness. But if genuine care and concern for the coachee is not at the forefront of what the coach thinks and does, then he or she is definitely in the wrong job.

4

The Achievement Matrix: Processes and purposes of coaching

So far we have looked at the interactional self and the choice cycle as separate constructs but the idea at the heart of these concepts is unitary: the self in time, with others and itself, as it encounters the three modalities of the choice process. So what happens if we combine these two three-stage constructs into a single, three-by-three matrix? The answer is the Achievement Matrix, a multivalent model that provides further insights into the reality of human choice and what it takes to coach executives successfully.

The Achievement Matrix operates at several different levels, which we will explore in this chapter. Level 1 is an overall account of the interactional coaching process, providing a picture of the process of a typical coaching assignment and, by extension, some of the different courses that coaching may follow. Level 2 provides a guide to identifying and locating specific coaching purposes, issues and situations and relating this to the coaching process as a whole. These two levels are illustrated in Table 4.1 (with Level 2 in italics).

In its most extended form the Achievement Matrix, as well as offering a reminder that the choosing process is always a totality, functions at two other levels:

- Level 3 is an outline description of the individual skills and abilities involved in successful choice transformations, amounting to a schematic account of the expertise necessary for achievement at work.
- Level 4 is a broad model of psychological and behavioural change that represents the change process in three

Table 4.1 The Achievement Matrix (Levels 1 and 2)

Choice cycle stage	Time	Self	Others
Identification (*Possibilize!*) Know what you want	1. Identify what you want and don't want (future-focus) *Coaching for vision and strategy*	2. Analyse and assess your values, self-reflectiveness and personality *Coaching for self-knowledge, insight and self-awareness*	3. Identify who you need to interact with and how *Coaching for interactional effectiveness and awareness*
Selection (*Probabilize!*) Choose what you want and learn how to achieve it	4. Manage uncertainty by managing time. Use your past and future to set your present *Coaching transitions and ambiguity*	5. Take responsibility for your choices and who you want to become *Coaching final choices Coaching confidence and personality biases*	6. Finalize your interactional strategy and work on your interactional skills *Coaching for communication and interactional skills*
Implementation (*Actualize!*) Achieve it!	7. Creating action-focus *Coaching flexible, action planning*	8. Implement your choices with resolution *Coaching action and inaction*	9. Build sustainable relationships *Coaching conflict Coaching 'failure' and relapses*

distinct stages: opening out, narrowing down and acting with closed (but not rigid) resolution.

The reader may ask: What is the value of such a model? The answer has to do with the complex, adaptable and multipurpose nature of coaching, which I referred to in Chapter 1. Coaching, it might be said, is like a liquid: it assumes the shape it needs in any situation. This protean quality makes it highly successful as a learning medium but presents a challenge when it comes to describing the practice schematically or accounting for it theoretically. Coaching might even be compared to the functioning of the human brain, which, as we now know, processes information both serially and in parallel. Coaching is a serial process, in that one thing follows another in each meeting and from session to session over time but, at any juncture in this process, a whole range of parallel choices and changes are also occurring. The result is that describing a coaching assignment before it starts, after it ends or at any point in between is by no means straightforward. Anything that clarifies this process, even at a fairly abstract level, can be helpful for the coach, the coachee and the coaching sponsor alike.

Level 1: General model of coaching process

The first value of the Achievement Matrix is that it provides an overview of the process of interactional coaching, which is broadly relevant to all types of coaching series, from short-form coaching (approximately 3–6 sessions) to mid-form (7–12 sessions) and long-form (more than 12 sessions).

Stage 1

Stage 1 generally corresponds to the first one or two sessions, where we identify who the client is and what she wants to achieve. This involves exploring the client's possible choices in the dimensions of time, self and others, which means exploring the client's trajectory towards the future – and her relationship to the past and present. Self-assessment is also foregrounded at this stage, particularly if the client has difficulty in developing self-awareness or identifying her own values and assumptions. It is also important to identify the people who are most important and influential in her working world and establish the skills and styles necessary to interact with them productively.

This pre-choice stage can be an exciting, creative and wide-ranging stage, often quite different from the more focused choice and action stages that will follow. Opening coaching sessions, in particular, are often memorable for both client and coach, a first encounter that can be moving and rewarding.

Stage 2

Stage 2 is about progressing to an action plan and developing the skills necessary to implement it. This is often where tough choices have to be made, as the client needs to take responsibility for what he wants to become. This can be especially difficult if it involves a step up from his previous experience and if it involves confronting preferred ways of behaving that now appear to stand in the way of progress.

Stage 3

Stage 3 is often the heart of the coaching series, where the coach supports and monitors the client's practical endeavours to turn his goals into reality. It is well known that many coaching changes happen in the 'here and now' of the coaching session but a good deal of them also occur in what might be called the 'there and then' of coaching. By this I mean the 99% of his working time that the coachee is likely to spend *outside* the coaching room. The ability to constantly to review actions prospectively and retrospectively over months or even years is one of the greatest assets of coaching, especially when compared to conventional group training where the foundations for change have to be laid down in a short space of time.

Working through the three stages is fundamental to interactional coaching and occurs, in one form or another, in the vast majority of coaching assignments. At the same time, it is worth emphasizing that it is often the variations on this schema that give a coaching project its unique character. Sometimes a coaching series will be focused almost exclusively on Stage 1, as a client struggles to define the parameters of her project, whereas in other cases the focus may be largely on making tough choices. Or it may be the action phase that is most problematic, where coach and coachee may have to wrestle with the opposition between the apparent perfection of the action plan and the difficulty of actually implementing it.

Patterns of change

The variability of coaching also shows itself in the very different patterns of change that can take place across the nine phases of the matrix. An even, incremental rhythm of change across the phases is one possible pattern, although often there is more change in the opening phases than in the later ones, as personal and interpersonal insights dramatically modify the client's choice landscape. Sometimes much of a coaching series is aimed at maintaining this initial change. Alternatively, there may be little obvious change for the client in the early phases and then a sudden breakthrough. This may come at Phase 5, when decisions have to be made, or at Phase 8, when an agreed course of behaviours needs to be implemented.

Another pattern of change also worth mentioning is the dramatic 'v-shaped' pattern of change, in which failed actions or a sudden loss of confidence can lead the client to relapse to an earlier stage and perhaps temporarily give up all hope of achieving his goals. This is often followed by a recovery, as he constructively reviews his situation with the coach. In the longer term, this experience can lead to profound changes in the coachee's awareness of his choices and his ability to put them into practice.

Level 2: Specific coaching purpose and situation indicator

The Achievement Matrix can also be useful for identifying some of coaching's many purposes and specific issues. Some coaching applications are likely to be fairly general and dictated by the role of the coachee, the nature of the organization or the interpretation of the coaching sponsor. Development and performance coaching, which we have already examined, often fall into this category, as does leadership and managerial coaching.

Table 4.2 **The matrix of coaching purposes**

Choice cycle stage	Time	Self	Others
Identification (*Possibilize!*) Know what you want	1. Coaching for vision and strategy	2. Coaching for self-knowledge, insight and self-awareness	3. Coaching for interactional effectiveness and awareness
Selection (*Probabilize!*) Choose what you want and learn how to achieve it	4. Coaching transitions and ambiguity	5. Coaching confidence and other personality biases. Coaching final choices and dilemmas	6. Coaching for communication and interpersonal skills and coaching around conflict
Implementation (*Actualize!*) Achieve it!	7. Coaching action-focus and flexible planning	8. Coaching action and inaction	9. Coaching sustainability and relapse Coaching 'failure'

Other coaching purposes may be more specific and emerge during the coaching briefing or the diagnostic phase of coaching. They may form part of the coaching plan, especially if it has multiple objectives, and will figure in the final evaluation of the coaching series. Although the Achievement Matrix should never be taken too literally, it can be useful in locating these purposes and issues, as illustrated in Table 4.2.

Phases 1–3

The initial identificatory or diagnostic stage may end up as the focus of the coaching series, with specific issues around identifying the client's personal and professional strategy or crafting a vision that will influence others. Sometimes, personal insight or self-knowledge may be the key purpose or the client's challenges in translating his aims into effective interaction with others.

Phases 1, 4 and 7

Transitions are a primary purpose in coaching, where a coachee is trying to adapt as quickly as possible to a new role or a new company or reacting to changes within or without the organization. This situation often involves coaching in the time dimensions of the self, when the goal is to deal with the gap between the past and the present, in the light of a new future. Helping coachees to handle ambiguity, a crucial competence for complex and senior roles, can also be partially seen in terms of our uncertainty around time.

Phases 5 and 8

Coaching in the personal dimension of the self is another area of specific purposes. A client's lack of confidence, for instance, is a frequent initiator of coaching, as are other personality biases. Coaching rational and emotional extremes, for example, may involve helping the client to develop empathy or more emotional self-control. Phase 5 is where final choices are made and sometimes this is the point where a client finds himself on the horns of dilemma, unable to decide one way or the other. Even after a choice has apparently been made, behavioural blockages can occur, which coaching may need to address.

Phase 6

Coaching in the dimension of others often involves work around interactional strategy, including interactional mapping. It may involve developing the skills necessary to put an organizational strategy into practice, such as communication skills, influencing and increasing interpersonal rapport. Helping clients to resolve the conflict situations that arise from relationships at work is another key application of coaching.

Phase 9

The final phase is about helping the client's ability to move from one achievement cycle to the next, especially by developing the optative awareness, which will help the client's choice-making in the future. Issues that may emerge here or be specified in advance by the coaching sponsor include coaching relapses, where a client has gone back on previous developmental gains.

Other specific purposes such as coaching creativity and stress can occur at any stage or phase of the Achievement Matrix, as they both involve fundamental aspects of choice-making. Stress may be experienced at specific stages of the work process, such as when making final choices or as a significant action approaches, or sporadically in a more generalized form.

Level 3: Achievement skills model

The Achievement Matrix has another extension, which came to light when I started trying to sum up what it is that clients gain from a successful coaching series and what qualities other potential clients already possess that make them unlikely to benefit greatly from coaching. In other words, how can we describe achievement, the ability to succeed in the workplace? This provides an opportunity to break down some of the individual skills involved in successful choice-making. Again, this will necessarily be schematic but is warranted if it can provide insights into an immensely fluid and complex process. It can be used for learning both within the coaching process and for those wishing to refresh their executive skills on a self-learning basis.

The nine achievement skills can be summarized as follows:

1 Know what you want and don't want.
2 Know who you are and how to analyse yourself.
3 Know who to interact with and how.
4 Manage uncertainty by managing time.
5 Take responsibility for your choices and who you need to become.
6 Develop your interactional skills.
7 Action-plan intelligently.
8 Implement your choices with resolution and flexibility.

9 Build sustainable relationships to renew the achievement
   cycle.

Level 4: Change model

The final application of the Achievement Matrix is as a
general model of change. As such, it describes the process by
which we move from possibility to reality: from the earliest
stages of the intention to act to the successful completion of
that action. As a change model, it inevitably has something
in common with other accounts of change, such as the six-
stage self-change model developed by Prochaska et al. (2006),
which moves from a 'precontemplation' phase through to
completion and recycling. It can also be seen as a model of
innovation in organizations, a process that often starts with
a mass of ideas that are then reduced to a small number of
development projects, out of which, it is hoped, a viable new
product or service will emerge. The process can be visual-
ized as a 'funnel of change', a movement from openness to
closure, as we explore the possibilities of action, narrow
down choices to the favoured few and then act on these
choices in a resolute but flexible way.

Part 2

Fundamental coaching purposes

5

Coaching for vision: Knowing what you want

Our choices about the future are among the most important choices we can ever make. Goals, objectives, purposes suggest that we are 'pulled by' the future rather than 'pushed by' the past and time has a huge influence on our moods. A vision is a design *of* the future and designs *on* the future, so developing an effective coaching vision can be fraught with difficulties. It can end up being too ambitious or too modest, too future-orientated or too influenced by the past, too self-centred or too concerned with others. So how can we help coachees to develop a situational strategy that is right for them? Often the answer is not 'out there', in the possibilities of the future or the claims of the organizations, but 'in here', in what the client most desires.

In this chapter, I suggest that identifying what the client really wants is the key to effective vision formation in coaching. We'll look at relatively straightforward visions and at situations when the dialectic of desire – the tension between what we want and what we don't want – can be much harder to unravel. We'll also address the question of whether coachees always have a sense of the future and examine the mechanics of goal-setting.

The self in time

The first cardinal question (What do you want to achieve?) is one of the most powerful any human being can ask. It is a question that is urgent, intuitive and immediately relevant to one's situation. At the same time, it points us inexorably towards the future, reminding us that desires have always yet to be fulfilled. Even if our desire is to retain what we have, or repeat pleasurable past experiences, this still expresses a claim on the future. 'Desire is a lack of being', says Sartre (1958: 88), the absence of something that has to come into existence in order to be satisfied.

It's easy to think of ourselves as being the product of our pasts. According to this model, we see time as a continuum, where we live in a present, pushed by what we have done in the past towards the future. Existential thinkers, by contrast, see the present as a product of the future rather than the past. We are pulled by the future rather than pushed by the past. 'Everything starts with the future', says Heidegger (2001: 159), in that our expectation of what is to come determines so much of the way we act in the present and influences the way we interpret our past. We noted earlier the effect that the future can have on our emotional state. Looking to the future optimistically can be a source of enthusiasm and positive motivation. If the future starts to look gloomy, our mood can drop sharply; and the absence of any hope can be the cause of depression. 'If there is nothing to look forward to, why bother to do anything?', a client once said to me, voicing the algorithm of negativity. Our attitude to time may be a source of realism, helping us to know exactly what we want, or a source of inhibition that severely limits our ability to achieve our desires.

Identifying the vision

From the very start, certain coaching clients are crystal-clear about what they want at work. 'I want to gain promotion', a client may say, or 'I want to run a company', 'I want to raise my profile' or 'I want to beat the competition'. For some coachees, the core motivation might be team-orientated: 'I want to help my team to grow' or 'I want to be part of a successful team'. For others, the key desire is part of a wider picture, for example, 'I want to change the way my professional field operates' or 'I want to serve my community'.

Sometimes the client's clear-sightedness is impressive. One coachee said to me: 'I want to be running a larger division in a year, be promoted to the board within two years and be running the company – or another like it – in five years.' Such clarity is not altogether surprising. After all, the desires that a client articulates in the opening session of coaching may be the result of many decades of choices. The choices you may make at school – deciding to study arts subjects, for example, as opposed to sciences – are likely to influence the kind of choices available to you when you enter the job market. The choices you make about going to university or embarking on a particular career will also have a bearing on your future choices. That's why it is useful to learn how and why a client made the choices that set him on his current track. Every choice has its history, therefore, which is not to say that this history is determining. Some people make very clear choices about what they want to do from the very beginning of their working lives, whereas others seem to 'fall into' careers, by which I mean that they made a choice that appeared to be random at the time but eventually turned out to be right.

Clarity of vision can also emerge from the organization, which constantly encourages its employees to channel their desires into pathways to the future. The forward-facing impetus of the contemporary organization can be seen in its corporate strategy (long-term, mid-term and short-term), in the objectives that are set for employees and, frequently these days, in the individual balanced scorecard that reflects these goals. The influence of the future is also evident in succession planning, which attempts to create a managerial pipeline, and in talent development, which accelerates the careers of promising employees.

Working with clients who have a very clear vision can seem like moving in a streamlined vehicle, unimpeded in its trajectory by obstacles or cross-winds. All the attention of the coach tends to turn to the next stage of the choice cycle – how to implement the strategy. Yet a word of caution is not out of place here. Even the most apparently clearly articulated vision can sometimes turn out to be a false track. Perhaps the client is only voicing what he thinks the coach or the organization wants to hear; perhaps he prefers any vision of the future rather than admit he is uncertain. Or perhaps he genuinely doesn't know that he doesn't know what he wants! Finding out just what the client really wants may also include separating fantasies from real, actionable choices. One simple way for the coach to test the resilience of a vision is by cross-checking with the other cardinal questions (Who are you? Who do you need to influence?).

It's also worth bearing in mind that designs on the future can also emerge from the past, perhaps in the form of a desire 'to rewrite history'. Choices that may feel right at one point in time can start to appear to be quite wrong at another. For instance, one highly successful, senior executive was haunted by a decision he had taken 25 years ago to forego a university education in order to help his financially stricken parents. His parents were long dead but this sense of educational loss persisted and gradually emerged as an integral element of his vision of what he still wanted to achieve.

Complex visions

Some clients bring more or less formed visions to the coaching dialogue. Others are much less clear about what they want in their working lives, so much so that answering this question may form the subject matter of a good deal of the coaching assignment. Part of the problem is that human desires come in numbers. We are capable of an extraordinary plurality of desires; it is just another consequence of our ability to conceive infinite possibilities in our interaction with the world. Inevitably these desires compete with each other for priority. Individually based desires, such as 'I want more recognition for what I do', may be at odds with more collective desires, like 'I want the team to do well'. The competition between a client's desires may be intense, a kind of psychological infighting that takes us to the heart of his situation.

One client told me, 'I desperately want to move up the organizational ladder' but also 'I want to spend as much time with my family as I do at the moment'. The more we explored the first of these desires, the more we came to the conclusion that realizing it would involve more time being spent at work, through more internal networking, client dinners and weekend travel. This was simply the type of organization he worked for. We looked at alternatives, moving to another part of the company, for example, or different ways he could be with his family, but in the end it became clear that the two desires were incompatible.

In such a case, the response is sometimes to fudge the issue and hope that somehow both desires will be fulfilled. 'To have our cake and eat it' is a powerful human tendency. Sartre (1958) calls this 'bad faith', although he does not suggest that we can ever entirely escape this predicament. It may be a natural response to the plurality of desires to try to achieve as many of them as possible, but this often brings about confusion and turmoil, even worse, it creates a kind of self-blindness as you attempt to persuade yourself that these competing desires are being fulfilled when, in reality, they are not. Sometimes a coachee may have to live for a good while with the clamorous confusion of her desires before making a choice, although merely articulating them is often enough to allow a vision to form.

Desires come in a negative as well as a positive form: 'what I want' competes with 'what I don't want'. For example, Miguel, a marketing executive, revealed that his vision was to move to the strategy department of his company but he didn't want to alienate his boss by openly declaring his ambition. I was keen to find out which of these two desires was the strongest. Miguel said that he was so grateful to his boss that he would never want to do anything that might indicate disloyalty to her. But as he talked he also began to hint that he was fearful of her anger, which could make his life intolerable if his move failed to materialize. In the end, Miguel decided to make the career move anyway but spent a good deal of time developing a secondary strategy for placating his manager.

Miguel's case shows that managing risk is in fact a hugely important aspect of our experience of the future. During economically good times, executives may take it for granted that they will always be able to retain their jobs or find equivalent posts elsewhere. This often increases the scale and scope of their ambitions, as reflected by their

coaching visions. An economic recession can have the opposite effect, reorganizing the executive's hierarchy of desires
and making job retention a much more important objective
than before.

Is what you *want* more important than what you *need*?
It may seem that wants and needs are in fundamental
opposition – and certainly can be experienced as such by
clients – but are they really so different? In many ways, this
is just another variation on the hierarchy of desires, as mediated by the reality of our situation. In an ideal situation you
may prefer to be a film star, but in the real situation in which
you find yourself what you want is to earn the necessities of
life, which often implies a less glamorous job. What I need is
generally what I actually want, even if in different circumstances I might want something else. Often the relationship
is mediated by time. For instance, a chief executive engaged
in the process of restructuring a company, which he found
quite distressing, said to me: 'What I really want is to find a
way I can give something back to society.' He then added,
'but what I *need* to do is finish this damn restructuring'.
Finding a way he could move from one desire to the next,
from the means to the end, became the theme of the coaching.

The importance of desire as a driver of choice-making
reminds us of the integrity of human thought and emotion.
In one sense, articulating future ambitions and career goals
can be seen as an intellectual procedure, but it is also an
intensely emotional process. The existential therapist Irvin
Yalom describes the powerful feelings raised by the question
'what do you want?' in a group context. 'Often, within
minutes, the room rocks with emotion,' he writes (Yalom,
1989: 3), and the emotional effect in coaching situations can
also be strong. In recent years, the concept of 'emotional
intelligence' (e.g. Goleman, 1995) has served a useful purpose
in asserting the significance of emotion in working life in
the face of academic psychology's prioritization of traditional, logico-mathematical IQ. But the importance of
emotion and mood has always been central to existential
thinking.

Being open to the client's emotional state is vital in
coaching, particularly in the early stages, because real

desires that are not identified at this point may go underground, so to say, and not emerge, if at all, until much later in the coaching process. Clarifying emotions can make a huge difference in revealing choices. 'My heart says this,' a client may say, 'but my head says that.' But which is which? Sometimes only through patient listening and questioning can the coach help the client to identify his true voice.

An absence of vision?

Do all clients have a sense of the future? In my experience, the answer is 'yes' even if this is not always immediately apparent. Sometimes clients may feel that they have no forward trajectory but only because they have been misled by the mystique that has always surrounded the word 'vision'. The fact that clients may have difficulty in articulating desires or goals doesn't mean that they don't exist. A client sometimes professes to have no goals or job aspirations, but when the coach digs a little deeper he is likely to find distinct aims and ambitions that have been either taken for granted by the client or dismissed into a sort of limbo of unarticulated desires. For example, Liam, a life sciences manager, told me: 'I am not a vision person, I don't have goals. I've never set a three-year plan, let alone a career plan . . . that's just not me.' However, when I asked him what he wanted to achieve in his department, he promptly replied: 'to keep doing what I'm doing . . . introduce our new product . . . perhaps take on a new team if I can win the resources'. To which I responded: 'And that's not a vision?'

On occasion, it can be useful for the coach to open the lens as wide as possible, as it were, to take in a wide vista of the client's deepest desires. Questions such as 'What would you do if money was no object?' or 'What would you do if you had one wish for the world?' take possibilizing to its most imaginative extremes. Such 'miracle questions', as they are called by solution-focused coaches (Greene and Grant, 2003), can have a powerful effect in moving from the possible to the probable. For example, one client found his professional calling by moving from his initial desire 'to bring about world peace' to his final choice to train as a disputes mediator.

Sometimes, a coachee's vision can be hard to identify because it expresses itself as a commitment to spontaneity. A coachee may have a deliberately carefree attitude to the future, pursuing a strategy of 'taking things as they come', moving from job to job 'until the right one comes along' or perhaps, in his personal life, 'sowing wild oats until it's time to settle down'. If this belief in spontaneity is completely authentic it may lead the coach to focus on more immediate, practical performance issues, but often it turns out to be something of a disguise. Take Ritchie, a newspaper advertising salesperson, who initially affected a winning insouciance about the future, including his promotion prospects. 'I'm not into any of that corporate stuff,' he said, 'I just want to have a laugh.' But once we delved a little deeper into what he wanted it became clear that he was anxious about his ability to compete with colleagues whom he considered to be more intelligent than him. Hence he had adapted a career ruse of quitting while ahead rather than being 'found out'. He was beginning to suspect, quite rightly as it turned out, that this strategy was not going to work for much longer. Out of his apparent non-vision, his true vision of what he wanted to achieve gradually emerged.

A client's apparent indifference to the future is often a form of self-protection. For instance, Catherine told me of her deep cynicism about everything connected to her energy company:

> I put everything into various enterprises which I was encouraged to do, and was let down very badly. More than let down . . . betrayed actually. I'm not going to make that mistake again.

Trying to block out the future may bring temporary relief but in time it is likely to jeopardize an executive's performance. When the future seems to disappear, motivation suffers. 'Running on empty' is one phrase that comes to mind to describe this state of mind, 'sleep-walking into the future' is another. Behind Catherine's cynicism was a dread of the future, dominated by the painfulness of disappointment and rejection and the fear of making further mistakes. Only when we identified a modest project to which Catherine felt able to commit herself did she begin to rediscover an openness to the future that enabled her to move forward.

Sometimes a graduated, one-step-at-a-time approach may be the best way to identify a client's vision. Here it is a matter of striking the right balance between goals that represent real stepping stones and goals that are so low they provide no real motivation. Consider Ted, a civil servant, who had a tried-and-tested strategy of setting limited work goals that he would gradually increase in ambition as he progressed. This plan of 'starting from the back', as he termed it, stemmed from his passion for long-distance running:

> When I run a marathon, I like to start from the back. That way I don't put too much pressure on myself early on. I don't get hassled at the start and I don't worry about being constantly overtaken. In the middle of the run and towards the end I start doing some overtaking myself. A lot of the blokes who start out quickly really suffer at the end and I can just breeze past them!

This hare and tortoise strategy worked well for Ted, who was often very anxious about the future. Nevertheless I had to ask Ted sooner or later: 'What might you achieve if you started off a little faster?' Contemplating this question, he gradually came to the conclusion that he was selling himself short and began to articulate a more ambitious vision for himself and his team.

Of course, like anything in life, a future-oriented attitude can be taken too far. Some executives seem to anchor themselves in an imaginary future, where success is guaranteed and the lessons of the past are irrelevant. This bland assurance is often the result of minimizing past mistakes and maximizing past successes. It is true that the line between courageous resolution and facile optimism is sometimes a thin one but the shallow belief that things will always turn out right, of the kind Voltaire (2005) so savagely satirized in *Candide*, rarely produces consistently positive results.

Throughout all this, we need to bear in mind that a client's stance towards the future comes in many varieties.

One useful difference is that between combinatorial and positional strategies, a distinction that originates in chess (Katsenelinboigen, 1997). Combinatorial goals are directional in that they are aimed at a particular job or role: for example, 'I want to be marketing director in the next eighteen months'. Positional goals are more subtle and less clear cut: for example, 'I want to develop my leadership abilities' or 'I want to be in the running for a top job when it comes up'. Often positional goals are about maintaining a plurality of choices. Organizational pathways are often obscure; after all, until a job actually becomes vacant all ambitions in respect of it are speculative. So executives are often keen to maintain their potential for promotion and can be extraordinarily sensitive to the currency of that potential. If an organization appears to have decided that an employee has 'gone as far as he can' in terms of promotion, this may indicate that it is time for him to look for greater opportunities elsewhere. Remuneration in general can act as a positional strategy, enabling an executive to 'buy time' in the sense of opportunities in the future. 'Money is like frozen choice,' a coachee once said to me, 'something you can always unfreeze when you know what you really want to do.'

Goal-setting in coaching

Once the client's vision has been established, the objectives for achieving this often emerge fairly easily in coaching. At times it is as though the objectives choose themselves, although it is worth spending time and effort in ensuring that they are as finely tuned as possible. In experimental conditions, organizational psychologists have shown that setting realistic goals can considerably increase task performance, as opposed to setting no goals (Locke and Latham, 1990). Setting unrealistic goals conversely can have a negative effect, particularly where goals are too high. It seems that if we come to a negative interpretation of a particular future (e.g. 'I will never achieve this task') we end up making less effort than if we had moderate goals or no goals at all. These experiments offer empirical support for the existential belief that our claims on the future have very precise and dramatic effects on our experience of the present. Interactionally, they also underline a crucial aspect of the relationship between the selection and implementation phases of the choice cycle: certain choices may look viable initially but turn out to be almost impossible to put into practice.

Setting effective coaching objectives is partially about being realistic about the number of goals that can be achieved. Probably for a short-form coaching series, one to three objectives are as much as can be achieved. For mid-form coaching, three to five objectives are viable, with more for a long-form coaching assignment of more than 12 sessions. Getting the balance right between certainty and uncertainty in the type of objectives set is also important. Directional objectives that aim at specific outcomes can run the risk of being too precise, in defiance of the uncertainties of the future. On the other hand, positional strategies, which aim at developing skills and being in the right place at the right time, can be too vague and ambiguous.

The time frame itself is another aspect of good goal-setting, as often this is key to establishing the right degree of challenge for the client. Setting a deadline for the following month has a quite different character from a deadline in six months. If a client has to achieve a task very quickly, this may necessitate some very fast decision-making. This may be just what she needs to spur her into action or it may be so pressurizing that she is unable to respond. A longer deadline may be what she needs to measure her performance or something she will constantly put off. So agreeing deadlines that suit the personality of the client is vital. 'Get on with it' and 'take your time' are two of the most powerful motivational phrases in the English language, but which to use and when? This is the real challenge!

By way of example, let's look at the coaching objectives that Alex, a manager in financial services, initially wanted to set for our 12-session series:

- Doubling the revenue of his team within six months.
- Making several important new hires.

- Building new customer relationships.
- Starting a new cross-divisional project.
- Doing something about team morale.
- Signing up for a financial course.

This list of goals – and this is only a selection – seemed to indicate an impressive level of ambition on Alex's part but I began to wonder if in reality it was an attempt to opt out of choosing. Sometimes choosing too many goals can be like choosing no goals at all.

The 'time fan' technique can be useful at this stage. This simply involves examining a phenomenon in terms of its present, past and future. Sure enough, when we explored Alex's present he seemed to be involved in a huge range of activities, only some of which were relevant to his real responsibilities and seemed to make it difficult for him to focus on his true priorities. 'I guess it's a case of headless chicken syndrome', Alex conceded. When we looked at the past, we found that Alex had a history of undershooting his targets, concealing a tendency to indecisiveness behind ambitious and opulent goal-setting. When we explored what was really important for him in the future, it soon became clear that until he hired several specialist team members, any other progress would be impossible.

The result was that we decided to focus on just two goals initially – new recruitment and prioritizing Alex's everyday activities. He actually seemed relieved by the clarity of purpose this brought him and he made rapid progress on them. In time, we were able to address Alex's other original objectives and by the end of the coaching project he had achieved most of them. Just as significantly, Alex began to develop much greater insight into his own ways of choosing. This enabled him to live his present in a more constructive, forward-facing manner, with what Heidegger (1962: 356) would call 'anticipatory resoluteness'.

6

Coaching for self-knowledge and self-awareness: Knowing who you are

'Knowing others is intelligent/Knowing yourself is enlightened', says the Tao Te Ching, written around 2500 years ago (Lao-Tsu, 1993: 33). It is a view that is endorsed in our own time by 'multiple intelligences' psychologist Howard Gardner (1983), who sees the capacity to explore one's 'intrapersonal' life as an important form of intelligence in its own right. Interactional coaching would put it this way: interacting with others is a key to executive success but how you go about this ultimately depends on how you interact with yourself. Your way of analysing yourself is fundamental to what you choose to make of yourself and the world around you. Without the ability to examine your thoughts, feelings and values, your capacity to achieve what you want at work can be haphazard and fitful.

The usefulness of accurate self-analysis was underscored by one client, in discussing the longer-term effects of his coaching:

> The biggest thing I got from coaching was becoming more self-aware. I gained the ability to take stock of myself, to understand what's going on for me emotionally and intellectually, before I decide to act this way or that. Previously, it was all a bit of a blur.

There are several forms of self-analysis that can help the coachee to bring this 'blur' into sharper focus, as we'll see in this chapter. These include self-assessment through oppositional enquiry and emotional analysis, examining your self-dialogue and identifying your personality biases. We also look at the different levels of individual consciousness and how these can interact in bringing about successful change in coaching.

Facilitating self-analysis

A useful way to begin the process of self-analysis is by asking the client: 'How well do you think you know your-self?' Some clients respond positively to the question in a way that leads on to a discussion of their personal and professional strengths and weaknesses. This response suggests that a client is reasonably well able to bring to reflection his innermost thoughts, feelings, values and personality preferences and the factors that influence his interpretation of the world. This is likely to increase his chances of making informed choices, especially in unfamiliar situations.

In other cases, clients immediately admit that they have little self-awareness; or they may claim to know themselves but in a way that turns out to be only partial. In both situations, it is likely that the coaching needs to address the issue of self-reflection and often this is the primary reason why the client has been referred for coaching. Nor does knowing what you want necessarily imply self-awareness. Clients sometimes have a clear sense of what they want to achieve at work but no real idea of whether they possess the personal or professional qualities required to achieve it.

The personal dimension of the interactional self can be compared to an inner landscape. It is a teeming emotional and intellectual environment, shaped by desire, where we find likes and dislikes, loves and hates, inclinations and disinclinations, as well as indifference and neutrality. Some of our beliefs, values, principles and ideas about right and wrong have been consciously chosen; others have been acquired less consciously, from our culture and our upbringing, from influential people in our lives and other experiences, including work experiences. Some of them are consistent, forming more or less predictable patterns, whereas others are unpredictable and inconsistent.

Forms of self-assessment

How can the coach help to identify the client's unique view of the world? In one sense it is simple, because everything a client says, including what she conveys by means of her non-verbal communication, is a potential form of self-assessment. Her stories, interpretations, favoured phrases and metaphors can all shine a light on her values. The client's self-narrative can be particularly revealing. For example, some coachees exclusively focus on work-related activities; others may talk about anything but work, preferring to talk about their families, their friends or their hobbies. Narrative choices of this kind can open a valuable window on the client's world.

Many forms of oppositional enquiry can also be useful in identifying a client's values. For example, the 'I am/am not exercise' can be one way to help a client identify the adjectives that define him, positively and negatively. A client may respond to the first part of the exercise by saying, 'I am . . . intelligent, fair, ambitious and cautious'. In completing the 'I am not . . .' sentence he reveals the opposite adjectives, such as 'unfocused', 'competitive', 'self-indulgent' and 'reckless'. Each of these oppositions has its story to tell. For example, the way 'intelligent' is contrasted with 'unfocused' could suggest a valuation of discipline and single-mindedness above creativity and flair. The contrasting of 'fair' to 'competitive' perhaps indicates a team-orientated approach rather than individually centred values, and so on.

Oppositional enquiry can uncover conflicts between a client's desires and their values. These self-divisions sometimes have their origins in the organization and its culture. One client in the media complained of the way in which his company thwarted his creativity by constantly imposing stringent budgetary controls on his work. This soon led to a much wider organizational dilemma, which was at the heart of the company's desire to be a creative leader and yet protect themselves from a succession of loss-making ventures that threatened their economic survival. Such choices and dilemmas are often at the heart of an organization's culture (Hampden-Turner, 1994).

Not infrequently conflicts between values can derive from a national culture or religion. For example, Samir, who initially expressed enthusiasm at the idea of leading a project in a highly competitive situation, became disheartened the more he revealed what he called his 'traditional Hindu values', which emphasized the importance of cooperation, the family and putting the group before the individual. Only when we explored this further did he begin to realize that he had always separated his Western-style business beliefs from his personal, religious and family values. This 'creative inconsistency' enabled him to start to identify his real aims at work.

Emotional analysis

It is easy to fall into the trap of thinking that self-analysis is only a cognitive process, but emotions often offer the shortest and most direct route to self-understanding. It can be illuminating for the coach to know, for example, which feelings the client most often experiences at work. Exhilaration, frustration, anger, boredom, anxiety and regret – each of these emotions carries a narrative that is potentially full of meaning and resonance. This narrative can unfold at speed. Emotion – the word's Latin root means 'movement' – brings the prospect of rapid progress towards self-understanding, as long as the coach does not provoke the coachee's possible anxiety around expressing and exploring feelings.

A sensitive method of introducing emotional analysis is to ask a client what motivates and demotivates him at work, as the concept of motivation is well recognized as a key to high performance at work. Another effective and relatively unintrusive way to discuss emotions is for the coach to ask the client to elaborate on her explicit emotional references, for example when she expresses disappointment, frustration or anxiety. Her non-verbal communication is also significant – a quick swallowing or choking sound, which indicates suppressed feelings, or perhaps a more obvious welling of tears. Indeed, the coach needs to be on the look out for emotional cues and be prepared to probe, not aggressively but with sympathetic curiosity, in order to unfold the layers of meaning that often reside in these affects.

Strong, recurrent emotions often take us to the heart of the client's self-interpretation. Exhilaration may reveal when she is really at her best, though perhaps without realizing it. Anger and frustration may indicate the main obstacles to success. Jealousy may reveal what the client most wants to be, while fear and dread uncover the situations that she will do most to avoid, perhaps to the detriment of her ambitions. Several times, for example, I have come across highly talented executives whose dread of public speaking has led them to curtail their career ambition and even deliberately turn down promotions that would involve additional public speaking.

But if emotions can reveal the truth, they are often equally effective at concealing it, which is why identifying and unravelling them can be so beneficial to the client. For Luke, an engineering manager, anger, mainly directed at his team, was a predominant feature of his management style. This anger simply reinforced his view that others were to blame for his unsuccessful team and blocked off any insights into the extent to which his own inconsistencies were contributing to his predicament. Carefully removing the screen of anger revealed some obvious steps for him to take in rebuilding his relationship with his team.

Self-dialogue

Self-dialogue is another way of looking at how we interpret ourselves. It is a metaphorical description of consciousness as a conversation with oneself. Self-dialogue is a kind of stream of consciousness, a flow of interactions with the world through which we identify and resolve the dilemmas and choices that confront us. It bears some similarities to what cognitive-behavioural coaches call 'self-talk' (Palmer and Szymanska, 2009).

Interactionally, self-dialogue is often explored in terms of linguistic tenses. The coach may ask the client how frequently she uses the future tense and what she tells herself about the future. This is likely to indicate how pessimistic or optimistic she is about her situation. How much does a client use the past tense? This may suggest how much influence their previous experiences have over them. And the conditional tense can be particularly revealing, as it relies on one event depending on another: for example, 'I can try to make it up with him but only if he apologizes first'. The conditional may indicate the real balance of forces of play in a situation.

Particularly important in self-dialogue is the imperative mood, the tense of commands and directions. The imperative indicates what you tell yourself that you have to do. For example: 'I'm supposed to be the last to leave the office', 'I'm always meant to be on time for meetings' or 'I have to be the most creative person around the table'. Often it is only when we look at the opposite of these imperatives that we begin to realize their true impact on the self. What happens if a client fails to live up to his own commands? One client may take the prospect philosophically (e.g. 'you win some, you lose some'); for another, the consequences may be little short of catastrophic.

Consider the case of Martin, an ambitious sales manager, who would repeatedly say: 'failure is not an option'. When I asked him why, he replied, 'using the word "failure" is like admitting I'm not up to the job and I can't deal with that'. In his mind, therefore, the stakes were always incredibly high, especially when it came to hitting sales targets. One consequence of this was that Martin began to become very devious, sometimes even altering his targets retrospectively rather than admit failure, which was extremely disorientating and demoralizing for his team. For him, the imperative to succeed was driven by such an overwhelming fear of failure that it threatened to turn into its opposite. The conversation he was having with himself was a kind of self-bullying, marked by a menacing voice that debilitated him more than it enabled him. Fortunately, identifying this hectoring voice was a major step towards Martin being able to moderate it, which eventually gave himself – and his team – a much better chance of succeeding.

Personality biases: Working with the ISO

The Interactional Style Outliner (ISO) can also be helpful at furthering self-understanding, as can formal psychometric tools. The ISO can give vital early clues as to a client's values and indicate the extent to which he is aware of the personality biases that influence his choice-making.

Shortcomings in self-awareness can manifest themselves in any of the five ISO dimensions. For instance, clients high in dominance may have problems in reflecting on their own motivations, seeing everything as a competition or struggle for power. Carmella, a senior accountant, found it difficult to analyse her thoughts and feelings accurately because she dismissed as weakness or triviality any experience that didn't appear to further her aims. Only by learning to regard some of these powerful inferences as legitimate in their own right did she begin to understand the subtle, rich and often mixed feelings she had about many situations. On the other hand, Al, an extremely supportive manager, ignored his own thoughts around asserting himself in team situations because he interpreted them as 'dictatorial' and 'disrespectful to the team'. This unconscious, pre-reflective bias made it difficult for him to listen to what he was really telling himself. In a sense, he was not fully privy to his own self-dialogue. Clients who are very low in self-confidence may also suffer a similar kind of difficulty in understanding their own inner life.

What about the respective strengths of introverts and extraverts at self-analysis? In my experience, introverts are more likely to be comfortable with introspection and more likely to spend more time in self-reflection than extraverts. Extraverts are more inclined to express their inner thoughts and desires through external references. One client, who could be extraordinarily subtle in discerning the motivations and behavioural characteristics of his colleagues, seemed to draw a complete blank when he was asked to describe why he had come to a particular choice in his life. Nevertheless, it would be misleading to conclude that self-knowledge is the natural province of introverts. In the right circumstances anybody can improve their ability to interact with themselves and engage in effective self-analysis or 'intro-action'.

Self-analysis and the levels of consciousness

What the client knows about himself is always important; but even more important, at times, is *how* he goes about achieving this knowledge. This is where it is so useful to be able to identify thoughts and values that lie outside the immediate grasp of consciousness. These are the elusive ideas, images or feelings that we think we know but can be hard to put into words. Often they represent assumptions or embedded values that are fundamental to the client's self-interpretation but in order to identify them we have to take account of the extraordinary complexity of human consciousness.

Sartre (1958) highlights two levels of consciousness: the reflective, that of which we are aware at any one time; and the pre-reflective, that of which we are not – or not yet – aware. This approach to psychoanalysis allows us to capture what is most valuable in Freud's insights into unconscious phenomena, while escaping the limits of his view of the unconscious as a separate realm of consciousness impenetrable to ordinary reflection or dialogue (Freud, 1963). In order to extend Sartre's formulation, we can add three others levels of consciousness, in the form of non-reflective, semi-reflective and super-reflective awareness.

The non-reflective level is the physiological or neurological functioning of the body and the brain, a level into which we can have no conscious access. Even so, aspects of our non-reflective bodily functioning can be influenced by our experiences, as evidenced by the many physical symptoms brought about by stress at work, such as headaches, stomach pains and insomnia (Cooper and Palmer, 2000).

The pre-reflective level of consciousness is the equivalent to Freud's concept of unconsciousness, except it is not seen as shielded from consciousness by some quasi-physical barrier. It is not conceived as necessarily having a regulatory function in preventing consciousness from accessing painful thoughts. Memories or other deep-lying thoughts and images can be accessed by conscious reflection but often this requires a sympathetic environment or the confidence to honestly examine one's own desires and reactions. At this level, we find 'embedded' values, assumptions and models of experience, which we have inherited from our social environment or our own interpretations. These have become so entwined in the fabric of our thinking and so taken for granted that it may be hard to recognize them. Disembedding these kinds of thoughts and holding them up to the light is often necessary for the client to understand what he really wants in any particular situation.

The semi-reflective level is made up of thoughts and feelings that seem to flit between full awareness and then disappear into pre-reflection. Often this is the case as self-exploration progresses and the learning process unfolds. This may be a function of the pressure that a client is under at work or the way existing patterns of experience reinforce embedded values, which make it difficult to retain these new insights let alone turn them into actions. It can take time – sometimes many years – to fully accept some aspects of yourself. This is especially true as even reflective values – beliefs that we readily acknowledge and use in our self-descriptions – may not be entirely stable and consistent, but form and re-form according to experience.

Discovering and retaining embedded thoughts can be a process that is full of surprises. For instance, Clive, a talented, outgoing executive in retailing, was constantly amazed at what he discovered about himself in coaching. It was a journey of genuine self-discovery for him, punctuated by statements of real amazement and pleasure, as even apparently unfavourable aspects of himself were revealed. Initially he used the phrase, 'another person has come out of the cupboard'. Gradually he accepted this other person was himself and, the more he did so, the more he changed into who he wanted to be.

Finally, the super-reflective level of consciousness is a form of higher self-awareness (referred to in Chapter 1) in which one can monitor one's own thoughts and experiences. This can be a state of high performance or 'flow' (Csikszentmihalyi, 1975), an almost paradoxical condition in which one is both relaxed and very alert. It also involves something akin to 'double-loop learning' (Argyris and Schön, 1978), in which one is conscious not only of an experience but also of what one is learning and how one can reproduce it in other situations. It involves the ability to step back from oneself or see oneself in action, as though from a third party. It is often most refreshingly evident in humour, the ability to laugh at a situation in a way that conveys a deeper truth.

From non-reflection to super-reflection: The case of Lisa M.

I'll try to illustrate the five levels of consciousness by the story of Lisa M., a corporate lawyer in her early thirties.

Non-reflective level

Early on in Lisa's coaching, she complained of frequent headaches and chest pains that her doctor had been unable to diagnose. She spoke about her boss, Adrian, very frequently but only in passing did she mention that she often had headaches after meeting him and had been physically sick on more than one occasion before meeting him. I quickly formed the impression that Adrian was a highly manipulative boss. Although I mentally bracketed this thought, the more I explored Lisa's situation with her, the more it became clear that Adrian had a habit of getting Lisa to perform tasks that he clearly should have been undertaking himself, and without giving her any credit for them. All the while, Lisa relentlessly dismissed her own abilities. To me, she came across as humorous and witty, but she reported that with Adrian she was always dour.

Pre-reflective level

When we began to explore why Lisa seemed unable to analyse what was going on in her interactions with Adrian, some of her pre-reflective assumptions and values started to emerge. For example, she had a strong belief in authority. In many ways, she was easy-going but she had such an embedded respect for those who are in charge that she found it difficult to articulate anything that might be construed as criticism of a superior. She also had a profound respect for professional knowledge and Adrian had a considerable reputation in the industry. Finally, she had a stoical belief, born of a long and difficult apprenticeship in male-dominated environments, that she ought to be able to deal with anything that a superior could throw at her, especially if he was a man.

Semi-reflective and reflective levels

By bringing these assumptions to the surface and articulating them (e.g. 'you should always respect people in authority'), Lisa began to bring to a reflective level what was happening in this relationship. But it took several sessions to consolidate these new insights. This was partially because her initials attempts to raise any questions with Adrian proved to be unsuccessful. Whatever subject she broached with him, he seemed able to deflect, talking her out of any prospect of change. In one session, for a while I had the distinct feeling that Lisa had completely forgotten our previous sessions and the insights she had gained into herself, but she suddenly smiled and talked about 'having another go'. This time at a fully reflective level, she prepared her case against Adrian as though it was a professional assignment and this produced a breakthrough. In our final session before a long break, Lisa seemed happy and relaxed and certain that things were moving in the right direction at last.

Super-reflective level

Seeing Lisa again after an interval of some months, I was impressed by her progress in her relationship with Adrian. At times there was a real understanding and respect between them, but at other times she would tease him, at a humorous level, in order to remind him that she 'knew his game'. She seemed to be able to play a kind of jokey school mistress role that kept him in check without being oppressive. Many a true word is indeed spoken in jest, in that humour can offer insights without apparent blame or accusation. 'I was only kidding . . .', she might say, when in fact she was not! Humour in this way can be super-reflective; it can also be semi-reflective, a moving in and out of reflection of something that is not yet fully 'owned' by the self. In this original way, Lisa seemed to have mastered the progression from non-reflective physical symptoms of distress through the pre-reflective and semi-reflective stages to a level of awareness that mixed reflection and super-reflection. The practical result was that she was much more knowledgeable about herself and her preferences and was able to make the very best of a situation that, at times, could still be quite challenging.

7

Coaching interactional strategy: Knowing who to interact with and how

In an age of increasing individualism we are repeatedly encouraged to regard the self as a discrete entity, but this would be a profound mistake. As Merleau-Ponty says: 'The social is a permanent field or dimension of existence. . . . Our relationship to the social is . . . deeper than any express perception or any judgment' (1962: 362). In other words, the interpersonal aspect of the interactional self is non-negotiable. Our involvement with others is always already there, whether we choose to acknowledge it or not. We are born, develop and live through others, and nothing better reveals the dense interconnectedness of our social relationships than organizational life.

Identifying who the coachee needs to interact with in his working world and how he should be interacting with them is central to the success of a coaching project. Developing an effective interactional strategy is at the core of all interactional coaching projects, either as part of the diagnostic phase of an assignment or as the specific purpose of the coaching. In this chapter, we look at ways to explore the coachee's interactional world, through questioning, interactional mapping and other forms of interactional analysis. We also discuss two common assumptions that executives hold about other people and how we can identify the interactional skills that a coachee needs to achieve his objectives.

Interactional questioning

The most direct way of entering into a client's interactional space is simply to combine the first cardinal question with the third: Who do you need to interact with in order to achieve what you want? This line of enquiry instantly starts to unravel the impact of other people on the client's working world. Typical responses are: 'I want to expand the project but my boss is blocking me . . . the management board doesn't allow it . . . the finance director won't release the budget . . . I'm being outmanoeuvred by my colleagues . . . my team resist doing what I want them to do', and so on.

Such statements bring us up against the realization that what you want in a social context has to be aligned with what others want. The dialectic of desire is even more complicated than we may have thought. What you want and don't want has to be reconciled with what others want and don't want, if you are to have a good chance of moving through the choice cycle successfully. Sometimes, the client's narrative and insights into her situation will be enough to form a picture of her relational world but when greater precision is needed a more comprehensive tool is called for. This is when interactional mapping comes into play.

Interactional mapping

Interactional mapping is a practical technique for developing the client's strategy in relation to others. It is a way of entering into the network of influence that surrounds the client and that will play a huge part in determining whether her goals will be realized. An executive's interactional map is made up of the individual stakeholders and constituent groups who directly influence his or her professional role. The extent of this map will vary according to the organization and her role in it. A chief executive may have more than a dozen different stakeholders or 'interactors', such as his chairman, the management board, shareholders, management team, the staff, customers (internal and external), regulators, City analysts, the press, and so on. A middle manager's interactional map may consist of her boss, her direct reports, customers, peers and junior colleagues, while the key interactors of a more junior executive may be limited to his boss and his customers.

What is crucial is not simply the extent of the interactional map but the relative importance of each of these interactors. It is the varying strength of these interactional dynamics that is crucial to understanding what the client needs to do to achieve his mission. To adapt George Orwell (1945), we might say that all working relationships are equal but some are more equal than others. It is these variable dynamics of influence that distinguish an interactional map from a simple organizational chart.

In interactional mapping, a coachee estimates her key interactions as two-way evaluations, combining her opinion of others with her estimate of their opinion of her. These estimates may be symmetrical (e.g. a client and her boss each have a positive opinion of each other) or asymmetrical (the client thinks favourably of her boss, but estimates that the boss has an unfavourable opinion of her). Such estimations will vary from role to role in the same interaction, so a direct report might be seen as 'brilliant with customers' but 'hopeless with his direct reports' or 'compelling when talking to her team informally' but 'poor when standing up to address shareholders'. Asymmetries of this kind often provide very clear indications of where a coachee most needs development.

The example of Mark L.

It is often useful for coach and client to jointly sketch out the client's key relationships. Figure 7.1 shows a schematic version of the interactional map of Mark L., a manager in a telecommunications company. Two things immediately stand out. Mark seems to have very good relationships with many of the people on his map. His direct reports seem to have a positive opinion of him, as indicated by their scores of H (high), as do his peers and his customers. But if these lateral and downward interactions are positive, the upward plane of the map is less positive. Jane, his immediate boss, appears to think well of him, a positive evaluation that Mark reciprocates. But Arjun, the company's new managing director, seems to have a poor opinion of Mark, as suggested by his L (low) rating. And although Mark highly respects

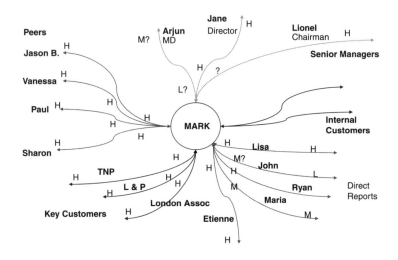

Figure 7.1 Mark L.'s interactional map.

the company's chairman, Lionel, he doesn't appear to know what Lionel thinks of him, suggesting a rather distant relationship. Since Mark's ambition is to consolidate his position in the company and expand his sales force, this lack of a positive evaluation by some of the company's principal decision-makers is a definite problem. Interactional mapping underlines again and again that lateral and downward influences, however necessary for accomplishing the job, are often secondary to upward influence when it comes to the decisions that most affect an executive's achievement goals.

Compare this with the interactional map of Mark's colleague and fellow manager, Jason B. (Figure 7.2), which shows some very different dynamics. First of all, Jason seems to have much better interactions with his senior management than Mark; they appear to be symmetrically favourable. Second, note the different range of ratings that Jason gives to his relationships. They tend to be all highs and lows, with very few medium ratings, perhaps indicating a dynamic, combative personal style, even a tendency to

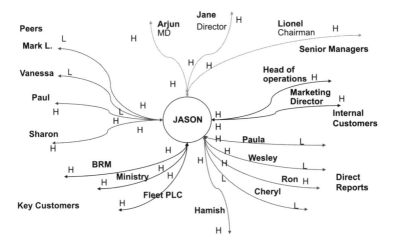

Figure 7.2 Jason B.'s interactional map.

judge everybody as being either for or against him. Contrast this with the more moderate and genial Mark, whose ratings are mainly highs and mediums. Finally, consider the rating that Jason gives to Mark, suggesting that he doesn't have a high opinion of his fellow manager's abilities. This view contrasts with Mark's own much more favourable rating of Jason and, crucially, his estimation of Jason's opinion of him. Since Mark and Jason are competitors for limited departmental resources, the fact that Mark seems to be in the dark about what his rival really thinks about him is perhaps another indication that he is likely to lose this political battle.

Of course, in the normal course of coaching it is highly unlikely that we could share one client's interactional map with another client, but the comparison illustrates a point that would probably emerge anyway, namely that Mark needs to open his eyes to what it takes to achieve what he wants. He definitely needs to improve his interactions with his senior management and perhaps be prepared to see that some of the people he tends to regard automatically as friends are potential blocks to his ambitions.

Others things to look out for on a client's interactional map are the resources that are available to her at work. What advice can she get from others? Who can offer her challenging views that she can trust? Who can offer her practical or emotional support for her project? Also important are the people who are *not* on the client's map. In other words, is the client interacting with the people who matter, as far as her goals are concerned? An executive may spend a good deal of time with like-minded colleagues who, although socially compatible, are irrelevant to her professional ambitions. And, going back to our example, note how many influential people Jason seems to be networking with who are absent from Mark's interactional map.

Getting the client to work on his own interactional map on a continuing basis can create ownership and permanent learning. This is important because coach and coachee alike need to be aware that an interactional map is a structure in a constant state of change. Changes will occur – partially as a result of the coaching itself – in the symmetricality of the interactions, as evaluations of, and by, the client alter. The very content of the interactional map can often change rapidly, particularly for executives in fast-moving, turbulent organizations. If, for example, a coachee's boss is suddenly promoted, this creates a vacancy that may represent a significant opportunity for the client or a potential threat. Either way, the issue is likely to move to the forefront of the coaching conversation.

360-degree feedback can also provide a valuable picture of interactional dynamics, by providing evaluations of the client by others. This may be collected through interviews by the coach or through a more formal version that provides quantitative data. Typically, in an interactional coaching 360-degree report, at least six rater categories are used: self, manager, direct reports, peers, indirect reports (staff who work regularly with the client) and stakeholders (internal or external customers). Whatever its form, as far as the interactional approach is concerned, 360-degree feedback is not just an organizational tool but a superb example of social interactionism in practice.

Interactional analysis

Another method of bringing out a coachee's way of inter-acting with others is simply by analysing some of the key situations that emerge from his description of his working relationships. This is likely to be an ongoing feature of any coaching project. Here we'll focus on three types of situa-tional interactional analysis, which relate to the past, the future and the conditional.

Retrospective analysis

Retrospective analysis is perhaps the most direct way of exploring how a client interacts with others. Often his account of a significant interaction in the past brings an immediate awareness of the issues at stake, some of which may not have been apparent at the time. For instance, Bradley, an executive in reinsurance, began describing in detail a recent contract with a customer but soon became completely absorbed by what he saw as the inefficiency of his supporting staff. He enumerated the stratagems he said he had to devise to cover up for his colleagues while selling the company's service. What had seemed like an interac-tional strategy aimed at improving customer relationships became much more focused on changing Bradley's interac-tions with his own back-office staff.

Anticipatory analysis

Exploring significant interactions with a client on a future-facing basis can also help to identify how she thinks about others and works with them. How clearly a client antici-pates events is revealing in itself. Some clients plan major interactions with meticulous attention to detail, whereas others let them happen more spontaneously. Examining what a client expects of an event is often illuminating. For example, this is what Anita, a corporate finance director, said of her imminent, off-site team meeting:

> The group needs to get a real sense of where we're going in the next 12 months. Things aren't going to be like they

were. Keeping a lid on costs has got to be our first priority but I don't want them completely demoralized by that.

As we talked through her team's possible reactions to this message, it became clear how she saw the alliances and groupings that made up the team. She kept coming back to two individuals, whom she used as a bell-wether for the morale of the team and as champions of any new strategies. Realizing how much she relied on these two team members took her by surprise. One of her conclusions was that she needed to become more inclusive in her approach and pay more attention to individuals whom she tended to ignore and whom she found 'cold and hard to put at ease'. This identified an important line of development for her in terms of her own interactional skills.

Conditional analysis

A third type of interactional analysis uses the conditional tense and focuses on what might be termed alternative histories. It's based on questions like 'What could have been different about this event?' and 'In an ideal world, how would this event have turned out?' Looking at other possible procedures and outcomes often reveals what is most significant in the client's current interactions. For example, Kelly, an advertising manager, said she was constantly 'hijacked' by the sudden conversational switches of Grant, a 'difficult' direct report. Grant would move from the personal to the professional and back again in a way that confused Kelly and resulted in her never being able to give him the negative performance feedback he deserved. By looking at her ideal scenario of how things might have gone, we quickly identified her assumptions about the 'rules' of the relationship that she felt her direct report was 'breaking'. She was then able to articulate these rules the next time she met Grant and create a more positive framework for the review. In this way, rewriting scripts can rewrite reality.

Two major interactional assumptions

In the course of interactional analysis, the client's fundamental assumptions about other people are often revealed.

Unearthing these embedded beliefs is an important coaching task, as they are some of the basic units on which our interpersonal worlds are built. Two interactional assumptions are particularly common in coaching. The first can be characterized as 'Everybody is different to me'. This consists of the belief that other people are more confident, competent and assured than ourselves. This is a very pervasive belief and although, of course, it may sometimes be true, coaching reveals over and over again the doubts and anxieties that underlie the most assured and polished of executive demeanours. Helping coachees to see that others may not be as different to themselves as they may assume is often a positive tactic in promoting more effective relationships.

However, oppositional logic dictates that this approach always needs to be situation-specific. This is because the second common assumption about others, which frequently surfaces in coaching, is the flip side of the first. 'Everybody is the same as me' is a presupposition that simply universalizes our own values and emotions, as though everybody else in the world was a kind of clone of ourselves. This generalization masks the real differences that exist between individuals and can lead to real misinterpretation and misunderstanding. It can certainly be a key challenge when it comes to managing others. Take Omar, an inexperienced manager, who was frustrated by his inability to motivate Ed, one of his direct reports. Omar said to me: 'I can't understand why Ed isn't enthused by the more challenging work I'm giving him now.' 'How would you react in his situation,' I asked? 'Positively, of course,' he replied, 'I love this kind of work. Doesn't everybody?' This query opened up an exploration of just how different in reality Ed was from Omar. What Omar experienced as a stimulating challenge, his direct report seemed to experience as a mixture of drudgery and anxiety-provoking confusion.

Achieving a workable balance between the 'everybody's different to me' and the 'everybody's the same as me' views of the world is no easy matter. And, just to make things even more complicated, these two sets of assumptions can often be held simultaneously by the same person. Finding a viable personal dialectic here is vital if clients are to make the best of their choices in relation to others.

Assumptions are often formed as the result of specific experiences, which are then (rightly or wrongly) generalized to apply to all situations. We do this constantly, transforming our choices into habits. To some extent, this is useful in that it avoids having to treat every new event entirely on its merits and choose afresh hundreds of times a day. But habitual responses can be unproductive if they stop us seeing the world and its possibilities. When habits become so ingrained that we are not even aware of them, they can unconsciously '*pre*form' our experience of the world in a way that can seriously affect the ability to *per*form at our best.

Identifying interactional skills for development

Interactional analysis, in its different forms, usually brings into sharp relief the people the client needs to influence to achieve her goals. The interactional map can cut through the multiple goals and shifting priorities that surround their job. 'It helps you dispel all the hype and reveal your real targets,' as one client put it. One result may be identifying 'quick wins', interactions that can bring positive results with a comparatively small amount of effort, which can be the prelude to more significant changes. Another is to encourage the coachee to analyse her important working interactions before, after and while they take place. This is a priceless executive skill that can help to make sense of organizational life, which at times can seem like a constant flow of information-rich events with no clear direction or meaning.

Interactional mapping also helps to reveal the specific, practical skills and competences a client needs to develop in order to achieve her project. Often her comfort with the analytical process itself is a significant clue here. For some coachees, mapping comes relatively easily and they will be able to identify their network and assess their interactional strengths without too much difficulty. This suggests that they are reasonably comfortable and skilled at working with others. For other clients, mapping will be more of an effort and they may be surprised to realize just how much of their personal success depends on others. For some clients, mapping is a serious challenge because they find it genuinely hard to appreciate other people's point of view. This suggests that they need to work more on developing the ability to switch perspectives and see the world from another's standpoint.

Interactional analysis also pinpoints deficiencies in interactional skills. Recall how quickly it became apparent that the key problem for Julia T. was her inability to interact effectively with her boss, Jonathan, and that, in order to remedy this, she needed to develop new communication skills. Similarly, Mark L. realized as we examined his interactional map that he needed a radically different approach to his direct reports and that some work on his managerial coaching skills was called for. Other shortfalls in interactional skills that may emerge include the client's ability to exert personal presence in one-to-one situations or meetings, or to present or network effectively. In some cases skills deficiencies are due to a real lack of competence, whereas in other cases they are due to a lack of confidence on the part of the client, but the key question is whether the client sees such shortcomings as impediments to her realizing her vision. If she considers that it will be difficult to put her choices into practice without certain interactional skills, it will be necessary to address these.

Whether this skills development is conducted within the coaching project or outside it, through training or other types of development, is something that has to be agreed with the coachee. Having the opportunity to make these practical choices can help him to develop optative awareness. It is also important that the coach is not unduly influenced by these choices: what matters is not who leads the development but that it is accomplished. We'll return to this subject in Part 5 with specific examples of interactional skills development within the coaching relationship.

Finally, it is worth returning to the philosophy underlying interactional coaching to underline the importance of reciprocity in human relationships (Sartre, 1992). In my experience, what emerges from interactional analysis is the realization that people are different from each other in many ways but alike in seeking to realize their goals in the world, pursuing their desires and making choices. This insight can help to promote healthy competition in organizations, based on mutually respectful exchanges between individuals, whereas its absence can lead to the conflict, confusion and demoralization associated with unhealthy competition – a subject we'll look at in depth in Chapter 15. It is another reason why working within the interpersonal dimension of the self is so valuable, both analytically and practically.

Part 3

Coaching in the time dimension

8

Coaching transitions: The past, present and future

All coaching involves transition but many assignments are prompted by specific types of change. Typical transitions include joining a new company, promotion, a change of roles in an existing organization or changed priorities due to restructuring or new market sector conditions. An executive may be transferring from one type of industry to another, from the private to public sector, or returning from maternity leave or a sabbatical. In public sector agencies, a change in the Minister of State can be enough to send ripples of policy change throughout an organization, and global economic changes, such as the onset of a recession, can have an impact on the design of almost every job. In short, transitions are the very stuff of modern organizational life, where, as we are often told, 'change is the only constant'.

For the interactional approach, coaching transitions is a particularly significant coaching purpose, as it is intimately bound up with the phenomenon of time. In this chapter, we look at how temporality affects coaching in transitions and the importance of time-awareness in coaching in general, as we examine the ways in which the present, the past and the future can prevent or facilitate change.

The time of coaching

An existentially-based understanding of time sees it as a lived phenomenon that leads to the recognition of the power of the future in our lives. 'Everything begins with the future', claimed Heidegger (2001: 159), which doesn't mean that the past and the present are insignificant, merely that we have to understand time in relation to our forward-looking expectations. This subjective, experiential approach to time can give the interactional model different, and perhaps richer, insights into change than coaching models, which use the conventional concept of objective, clock time. Objective time is the time that chooses us, defining us by a standard measure. This, of course, is an important aspect of reality, which we would be ill-advised to ignore, but the concept of objective time can limit our ability to see the extent to which we choose our experience of time. This is partially a matter of becoming aware of the subjective variations in time, such as the seemingly endless seconds as we wait for an important announcement or the hours that appear to flash by on a productive day. We also choose time by how we organize ourselves in relation to getting the best out of the present, setting future projects and interpreting our past.

Objective time and subjective time constantly interact in coaching. An insight that changes a client's way of thinking that has persisted for decades may occur in a few seconds of clock time. Or sometimes a whole session may go by when it feels like little new has been revealed or achieved. Repetition, one of the least glamorous aspects of time, also has its place. Sometimes, in order to progress, the coach needs to remind the client of agreed objectives 'time and time again', or patiently return to unresolved dilemmas or mysteries.

Coaching's extraordinary adaptability is partially due to its temporal flexibility, which makes it quite distinct from other development forms such as group training, with its immediate, one-off format, or formal education, with its longer-term but rigid structure. Coaching has the ability to run both the sprint and the marathon, so to speak, working over a long extended period but accelerating whenever necessary. Urgent performance coaching may involve sessions on a weekly or fortnightly basis, whereas review sessions after a sustained coaching assignment may take place once or twice a year. When it comes to transitions, time-awareness is particularly significant, as there is often pressure on the client to adapt to a new situation in a short period of time. This can bring into sharp relief differences between the client's present, past and future.

Coaching transitions

In one sense, transition coaching is simply about getting the basics right: working through the choosing process from identification and selection to implementation. Often, establishing key priorities, highlighting potential alliances and reminding the coachee of his strengths and weaknesses can start to cut through the potential confusion caused by a radically new situation or role. Taking account of the changes in the client's interactional map is particularly valuable, as it is not only the unfamiliarity of many of the interactors that is challenging but also the sheer range of the new relationships involved. This is particularly true of transitions involving promotion, where the executive may find herself with a much larger array of constituents than before. The typical senior manager's first 100 days in a new role is a paradoxical mixture of listening to as many people as possible and learning from them how the new organization works, while simultaneously exerting a firm leadership presence and offering the beginnings of new vision. This is not an easy tightrope to walk.

Executives in transition often stumble on the step between the past and the present and the changes of meaning, relationship and working style that it involves. This negative experience may be immediate, causing instant panic or despair, or it may be more gradual, as the gulf between the executive's world and her new situation slowly opens up. In both cases, it may be that the executive has to become, in certain respects, a different person in order to perform her new role, a shape-shifting of values, feelings and behaviours that can be profoundly challenging.

The paradox of change: The case of Will P.

One of the obstacles that most frequently appears on the path of transitions is what might be called the paradox of change. We want to change but we want to stay the same; we want to move to the future but to retain the security and achievements of the past.

This paradox is particularly common in organizations that are going through rapid change, as Will P. discovered. He was an experienced financier who was recruited from a progressive bank into a more traditional bank to bring about much-needed change. Will was initially very clear about his role – 'to drag this place into the twenty-first century', as he described it – but over time he became frustrated by the obduracy of his new employers' existing values and ways of working. One of the things he found particularly annoying was the way poor performance seemed to be tolerated. He cited the case of a colleague who was promoted 'for doing nothing', which Will complained about overtly to his peers in a way that violated some code of silence that the bank still respected. Worse still was Will's handling of the internal publicity over a breakthrough deal that he had succeeded in bringing to the bank. Instead of celebrating the deal widely in a way that would have encouraged others, he publicly criticized the legal department to senior management, suggesting that its shortcomings had reduced the overall profitability of the transaction. This had prompted increased resistance to Will's way of working and raised a question mark over whether he was the right person for the job.

Will said that he 'instinctively' felt that his values were right. 'It's wrong to condone poor performance,' he stated, 'it encourages sloppiness, complacency and injustice. It's what I thought I was brought here to change.' But the more we talked through the consequences of his overt stand on these points, the more he realized how counterproductive it was to his cause. He was not changing the culture; if anything, he was reinforcing it. He was seen as a disrespectful loudmouth, stepping beyond his remit and an 'outsider', even by some of those who saw the need for change. What had been right in his previous organizational culture was often seen as wrong in his new situation. In short, he needed to change his way of choosing by modifying his values of 'right' and 'wrong'. A lot of this came down to time. Will's beliefs may have been justified but his sense of timing was poor. For example, his criticism of the legal department could have taken place quietly, after the celebration of the deal. More importantly, Will had misinterpreted the pace at which it was possible to achieve change in the bank. He concluded that he needed to be more patient and artful:

It's partially a waiting game here rather than a mad dash for the line. If I'm to make a go of it, I need to change some of my priorities. I'm not abandoning my beliefs about poor performance but I'll have to go for subtle raids when the time is right rather than an all-out frontal assault!

As a result of becoming aware of the choices he was actually making and modifying them through a new time frame, Will's career in the bank began to take an upward turn.

Focusing on the present

Inevitably, one of the temporal challenges thrown up by executive transitions is the present. The reality of everyday work can be so powerful that it is difficult to get into a balanced, forward-facing mode that also does justice to the past. Learning to manage the present is crucial if an executive's objectives are to be achieved. Yet such is the rapid pace of modern life in the workplace, where 'back to back' meetings have become commonplace, that some executives seem to have surprisingly little understanding of what they do day to day. 'Not enough hours in the day', was a favourite retort of one client, who seemed to live in the 'nowness' of the present where everything had to be done immediately, which often meant it was not done at all. This is why analysing everyday activities, even getting a client to log her daily tasks, can be illuminating, in transitions and elsewhere. It sometimes points up a sharp distinction between the executive's real agenda and that of other people. Clients often seem to find themselves cajoled by others into tasks that prevent them from realizing their own potential. It can help to enquire: What will happen if an activity is not performed? The answer is often surprising, as with one client who mentioned an arduous report that he had been asked to prepare every month but, on further investigation, it turned out that nobody had actually read it for over a year.

Making time is one of the priorities in coaching transitions. This means allowing the client to step back from the everyday and review what is important in the present, the future and the past, an activity particularly appreciated by clients. This allows for a separation of what is urgent from what is important, which often corresponds to the difference between activities that need to be dispatched because of immediate concerns and those that point towards longer-term developments. Identifying this distinction is important for the client's action planning and general state of mind. As Heidegger (1962: 463) puts it, the person who is always busy is 'constantly losing time' but the person who lives his present authentically 'never loses time' and 'always has time'.

Another effect of time in coaching is the way goals seem to be forgotten by the client from session to session. In the apparent session-by-session continuity of the coaching series, it is easy for the coach to underestimate the richness and potential disruptiveness of the intervals between sessions, like the black area separating images on a reel of movie film. In other words, the real time of the coach can be very different from the time of the client's working life, consisting of hundreds of busy hours of work in between coaching sessions. Yet, intriguingly, when coach and coachee are in the same time stream, what happened in a previous conversation, perhaps several months before, can seem more real and present than something that happened minutes before the session began.

The strength of the future

If the present can sometimes obscure the future, the opposite can also be the case. Some people can be so driven by powerful expectations that the present appears like a mirage, a meaningless chaos, that will rapidly pass away once the future takes shape. Indeed, the present may seem like a seductive trap that has to be avoided at all costs if change is to be allowed to happen. But if we fail to respect where we are now and where we have been, it may be impossible to ever make the leap to where we want to go.

Consider the case of Gary, who was struggling to make a transition to a new management role in his data systems firm. Gary's positivity about the future was truly impressive. He painted a picture of his department after his restructuring in the most glorious and vivid colours. But his vision appeared to be unaccompanied by any detailed planning or thoughtful assessment of the personnel involved. When we looked into his career narrative, a recurrent theme seemed to emerge of Gary rushing into operational projects in a whirlwind of enthusiasm. This was infectious, even to the point of persuading older hands to go along with something they may have been uncertain about. But the results that were promised were rarely delivered and Gary hinted that his ability 'to bale out at the right time', together with his grandiloquent descriptions of his achievements, was all that had enabled him to keep his reputation intact.

Why was Gary choosing to plan his new role like this? Once we started looking at the concrete details of his departmental project, part of the answer seemed to become clear. The clue was not so much in what Gary was saying, as in his emotional demeanour and vocal tone. I felt I needed to put this observation to him and said: 'Gary, you seem bored by all of this.' He nodded his head in agreement. In fact, his exuberance dropped so fast that, for the first time in our sessions, he soon lapsed into a kind of sullen silence. 'Emotionally, I find this all so draining,' he said after a pause, 'there are just so many things to sort out at this micro-level, so many choices I have to make. After a while, the big picture disappears.' This was at least a starting point, as Gary had never fully admitted this to himself. Invoking the future, I asked him to imagine what it would be like to have to 'bale out' again? He admitted that it was not an attractive prospect and added: 'I'm not sure I'll get away with it this time.'

For the next couple of sessions, we stuck with his preparations but found ways in which he could endow them with some of the excitement he saw in 'the big picture'. Using conditional analysis, for instance, we drew a hypothetical line between possible management structures and possible future outcomes and this seemed to help the present and the future come together for Gary. Although planning remained a chore for him, his mastery of detail improved significantly. For example, he began choosing personnel with much more deliberation, favouring staff who complemented his own skills rather than duplicating them, as had been his preference in the past. In time, much of his enthusiasm for his new role returned but now with a more solid foundation.

By contrast, look at how another client, Sean, negotiated a transition. Sean was exceptionally time-aware and used the future, in combination with an honest and penetrating analysis of his past, to help him make a major career choice. He was in his mid-sixties, a successful businessman who had decided to change direction entirely and train as a nutritionist. Some people would be overcome with feelings of futility at the thought of being almost 70 by the time they were fully qualified for a new role, but Sean was absolutely determined to persist with his training. What kept him going, I asked? He replied:

> You know it's quite simple. I keep thinking of how old I felt when I was younger! I remember when I took my MBA, for instance. I felt I was positively geriatric and kept thinking, I should have done this in my twenties. I was 41, for God's sake! That seems like a teenager to me now! I don't want reach the age of 80 or 90 and think why the hell didn't I do what I wanted to do in my sixties? If my time comes before that, fair enough, but I don't want to spend my old age thinking 'what if?'

This 'future point' technique, whereby you imagine a precise moment when you reflect back on your life – a life you have not yet lived – can be very effective. It can put order into the often bewildering maelstrom of time, enabling you to get in touch with what you really want.

The power of the past

Not everyone is able to use the past as skilfully as Sean in making major transitions. The past is often a formidable threat to successful change. It can exert itself over the present, dominating transitions to the extent that choices are diverted from action and turn back on themselves. And yet, as Sartre (1958: 499) observes, 'It is the future which decides whether the past is living or dead', implying that it is our goals and intentions that determine which elements of the past are relevant to us in any situation. In this sense, the past doesn't exist 'in itself', purely objectively, but as a field of choices. Past choices are always available to be rechosen. An everyday example of this is the way a person's curriculum vitae can change according to the job he is applying for. Experiences and qualifications that may be extremely relevant for one job (i.e. one future intention) can be utterly irrelevant to another. The way we interpret the past is what really matters, especially the way we choose to categorize our experiences as negative or positive. In this respect, the past can be an accelerator or a brake.

Sometimes the influence of the past on transitions can be relatively easy to identify in coaching. For example, Leslie, a regional director, was starting to implement her fashion distribution company's radically new strategy. She wanted to talk through her imminent announcement of the closure of a branch in the North of England. It quickly became apparent that she was anticipating this event with dread. 'I keep thinking about the people we're going to lay off.' 'I've known some of them for twenty years,' she said sadly, shaking her head. 'The branch manager started as my PA.' But as we talked it became clear that in this particular situation the prospects of most of the staff were far from gloomy. Many would be redeployed to other regions, if they so chose, although unemployment in the area was much lower than the national average, so local jobs were likely to be available. Some staff would be offered generous redundancy packages. After outlining the redundancy conditions, Leslie said:

You know, everybody lives in fear of being let go but I can only think of a handful of people over the years who haven't done well by it. It helps a lot of people make choices they couldn't otherwise make.

Leslie's nostalgia for the past gradually transformed into a sense of the opportunities awaiting many of the staff in the future. In the end, she made the announcement to the branch in a sensitive but fundamentally positive, forward-looking spirit. This, combined with her exceptional personal commitment to her staff, turned the entire episode into something far less dreadful than she had initially envisaged.

Of course, for coaching, past patterns of choosing can be a rich source of information and learning, as long as these patterns are relevant to the present. Past choices may tell us something important about a client's style of choosing. For instance, compare the client who said she embarked on her current career 'as a last-minute decision' with another coachee who claimed he'd never given his career any conscious deliberation: 'My dad was an engineer, so I suppose that was good enough for me.' Negative decisions in the past, or missed opportunities, can also be significant, as they are often a source of motivation in the present. The desire to overcome past mistakes can be a cogent driver of change. When the future itself seems too obscure, too difficult to believe in, too lacking in positive signs, then the past can be inspirational. 'I never again want to be in the position of being totally beholden to others,' said one client about a particularly harrowing episode in his working life. 'That's what keeps me going today.'

Sometimes, though, the impact of negative interpretations of the past can be extremely hard to handle. Failed choices in the past can hijack the future, making it impossible for people to go through the achievement cycle. Negatively interpreted past experiences may intrude deep into consciousness, making negative desires (e.g. 'I don't want that to happen again') dominate more positive desires ('I really want to do this'). A disastrous job interview, for example, may be transformed into the assumption that 'there is no point in applying for jobs'. This attitude may become so embedded that it sinks to a pre-reflective level, exerting an influence over many of the person's choices, even though he is no longer aware of it.

Releasing the grip of the past: The case of Graham J.

The influence of the demons of the past is evident in the case of Graham J. He was an executive in his late twenties who had recently been promoted to run an ambitious, high-profile project in a thriving video games company. He was finding it extremely hard to make the transition to his new role, feeling no sense of control over the key decisions he was making. He said he was being constantly undermined by his direct report and former peer, Marina, who was resentful at not having been appointed to lead the project, even though she was far less qualified for it than Graham. What seemed to prevent Graham from asserting his authority in his new role was the fear of repeating some of the mistakes he felt he had made in past projects. This made it easier for someone as ambitious as Marina to outmanoeuvre him. 'I half-wish that she would just take over the project and have done with it,' he told me, but then admitted that such an outcome would be a bitter humiliation for him.

Ten minutes into his life narrative I was struck by how Graham seemed to be haunted by past failures. This went back to his childhood, where he always appeared to be looking backwards at something that he had failed to do, rather than forwards to what he was actually achieving. For example, he remembered the 'debacle' of a school drama he produced but not his consistently excellent academic and sporting results. He generally played down his qualifications and talents and had often applied for jobs that were lower than his experience merited, in order to avoid the possibility of rejection.

In coaching, he focused repeatedly on two traumatic experiences of project management in previous companies. When we looked at these 'massive screw-ups', as he called them, it became clear that in both cases he had been put in charge of major projects without adequate preparation or support. Nor were the projects complete failures, although they didn't achieve the very demanding targets that were set for them.

Coach: It seems to me you've been dropped in the deep end.
Coachee: Yes but isn't that the way you learn to swim?
Coach: Sometimes.
Coachee: I should have been able to cope.
Coach: The trouble is that even if you don't drown, you generally don't learn to swim in a particularly efficient or elegant way. In fact, you learn to keep your head above water and that's about all. Which is exactly what you did.

Re-interpreting these past events didn't magically make the pain that Graham felt disappear but it did start to throw up some new possibilities for him. He realized that he would never place a subordinate in the kind of position he had been placed by previous bosses. He also saw just how much these managers had relied on him, although they had never conceded this. In due course, he was able to disentangle bad luck and bad management from the genuinely poor decisions that he had made in these projects. There is no way of reversing bad choices in the past – which is one of the reasons why making decisions can cause us such apprehension in the first place – but we can immunize ourselves from some of the harm those choices can cause in the present.

As Graham began to see how his unrealistically high standards had held him back in the past, he was able to look at his present project more openly and see that in reality it was going fairly well. This also brought it home to him just how much of an impact his troublesome direct report was having on him. Marina also seemed to be fixated by the past and unable to deal with her failure to get Graham's job, although, unlike Graham, her disappointment expressed itself in aggression and self-pity. Graham embarked on a process of listening to her grievances, sympathizing with her situation and then firmly reminding her of her actual position within the company. He asked her to 'let bygones be bygones' and focus on what they could now achieve together, a fact he related to me with an ironic smile. After some difficult exchanges, Marina seemed to fall into line behind Graham's vision of the project, which enabled him to assert his authority in ways that were more productive for both of them. As the project moved towards a successful conclusion, Graham's past, although occasionally still a sore point with him, gradually became what it always had been: history.

9

Coaching ambiguity and uncertainty

'Ambiguity is of the essence of human existence', Merleau-Ponty (1962: 169) argues, so we should not be surprised to see ambiguity and uncertainty arising in numerous situations at work. Occupational transitions are likely to contain more uncertainty than more established situations, because they contain so much novelty, but managing uncertainty is a continuous challenge for coaching. The interactional model sees uncertainty as an unavoidable aspect of our human condition as choice-makers in interaction and, as such, can be either positive or negative. It can be constructive as a source of creativity and productivity but destructive as a threat to stability and order. For coaching, the challenge is to help the client negotiate the personal dialectic between certainty and uncertainty and find a way to bring out the best in both of them.

In part, uncertainty stems from the unforeseeable nature of the future. Organizations attempt to reduce the uncertainty of the future by means of exhaustive forecasting and long-term planning, but often to little avail, as the largely unpredicted onset of the global economic recession in 2008 demonstrated. Executives can become fixated on targets and projections, to the point that these essentially speculative activities take on a weighty, thing-like reality. 'The mid-term objectives are sacrosanct', one finance manager told me confidentially, before admitting that every year for the previous five years he had had to change these objectives, due to 'unforeseen movements in the market'. Uncertainty is uncomfortable as it gives us a glimpse of just how complex reality really is. But trying to do away with this discomfort altogether, however tempting, can be dangerous.

In this chapter, we look at the effects of uncertainty on executives making the transition to new roles, including senior management positions, and how uncertainty can replicate itself like a virus. We also explore how coaching can help clients to find the personal dialectic that enables them to use ambiguity as a powerful, positive resource at work.

Uncertainty at the top

Uncertainty can be a major trial for people climbing the management ladder. From the bottom looking up, it seems that the higher one goes in the firm the more certainty there must be. Managers at the top appear to be more certain, in part because of their demeanour and in part because of the assumption that they have access to more information and greater authority to make things happen.

In my experience, however, the reality is often that the higher one goes in the organization, the more uncertainty appears to be the order of the day. A visitor even senses this in ascending a typical corporate high-rise building. On the lower floors, the space is carefully structured into precise cubicles and areas that neatly define everyone's working world. Moving upwards, we begin to encounter the reverential hush of the top floors with their wide corridors and capacious offices, offering commanding views of the surroundings. Here space is a privilege and a sign of status, but it also indicates a freedom that needs to be defined by its occupiers.

It is not only that decision-making at the top is more ambiguous and unstructured than anticipated; it is also that the specialist knowledge that an executive probably feels is responsible for his promotion now has to be supplemented by other expertise, particularly interpersonal and strategic skills. The result is that initially the new role 'doesn't feel like real work', as one client phrased it. What has happened is that ways of choosing that worked in the past are no longer effective. There is often either too much or too little information available, which makes decision-making at a senior level much more complex. Apparently clearly cut differences now seem blurred; primary colours are replaced by bewilderingly subtle shades and bold lines become fuzzy. Even evaluating whether a final decision was right or wrong becomes more drawn out over time and subject to many different opinions.

Often the most effective way to address uncertainty in coaching is by going through the basics of the choice cycle and the interactional self. Establishing what the client wants in the real situation in which he finds himself, spelling out his personal and professional resources, how he goes about choosing and working out his interactional map – all these processes are more important than ever when new uncertainties about the future open up. Helping to identify the novel choices that confront him and the unexpected opportunities that may have emerged can move the client towards a set of realistic objectives. For example, Lynne joined a publishing company in a senior position with an apparently clear remit. She regarded her job description as an accurate account of her new role but overestimated the degree of certainty it contained. Only after a good deal of confusion, self-questioning and silent criticism of her employers did she come to the conclusion that her job description should have read: 'Invent this job if you can!' Once she realized this, that's exactly what she proceeded to do.

In conditions of uncertainty, going through the stages of the choice cycle is particularly valuable because often a client's reaction to an ambiguous situation can be to make decisions that are either too risky or too risk-averse. Only by getting the fundamentals right can the true status of a choice be ascertained. 'I was looking for a totally new way to deal with this crisis', Pieter said, after a sudden deterioration in the prospects for his marketing firm. 'What I needed to rediscover was the calm, common sense that always worked for me but that's what flies out the door when something like this happens.'

'Learning to love the grey': The case of Sangita P. (continued from Chapter 1)

Coming to terms with uncertainty often calls for new ways of thinking, feeling and living in the world. This is

something experienced vividly by Sangita P., whom I introduced at the very beginning of this book and whose full story
can now be told. When I first met her, Sangita had recently
been promoted to the role of facilities director for a public
sector organization, while her boss was on maternity leave.
Unexpectedly, her chief executive embarked on a major
cost-cutting exercise and called for a comprehensive review
of the organization's numerous offices across the country.
Sangita was known for her reliability and her meticulous
knowledge of the agency's existing sites, which she said she
knew like the back of her hand. Now she had to come up
with a viable new strategy to dispose of some offices and
acquire others, which meant a wide range of interviews with
colleagues, property agents and suppliers.

Sangita's problems were apparent in her strained
features as she discussed how badly her preliminary plans
had been received by the CEO and his board. It seemed that
they had failed to understand her intentions, and when she
pulled out a voluminous preparatory document it was easy
to see why. The amount of detail she produced for every
element of her proposal was exceptional. 'I don't like uncertainty,' she said, 'I like things black and white, no loose
ends.' When we talked about her life she revealed her almost
obsessive concern with tidiness and order. Her desk was
immaculate, with never a pen nor a paper clip out of place,
and she said she kept her flat in the same condition. And yet,
with all this neatness around her, she was waking up in the
middle of the night panic-stricken at the thought of her next
day in the office, in a job she used to love.

Working on Sangita's communication style was a
priority. Helping her develop short, clear, headline messages
rather than the paragraphic utterances that were her stock
in trade seemed essential. Working oppositionally, I also
asked her to find instances at work where she herself was
irritated by too much detail. In the end, we kept coming back
to the degree of certainty she required in order to come to
conclusions and she repeated her point about needing things
to be black and white. I suggested that the space between
black and white was not as negative as she made out. 'There
are after all an infinite number of shades of grey in between.'

Rather to my surprise, Sangita seemed impressed by this metaphor and mentioned it several times in our sessions, as a kind of benchmark for her progress.

Time was a serious problem for Sangita. The future seemed to induce a kind of panic in her. She wanted to sort out every eventuality in advance, leaving nothing to chance. We analysed some meetings she had coming up and she unleashed a flurry of questions about what might happen in them. In part, she appeared to be bothered by the prospect of having to act spontaneously and make choices on the spot. In part, she feared criticism, not only from others but also from herself. Yet when we role-played an unpredictable meeting, Sangita coped perfectly well. Acknowledging this and realizing that she had not 'gone to pieces', as she had firmly expected, enabled her to start experimenting with less preparation and more openness in her workplace interactions.

We ran through different scenarios for her next board presentation. I suggested that the range of her colleagues' possible responses to her proposals was not necessarily a negative and could even be a positive. Sangita initially baulked at this but she reluctantly conceded that she could not predict how they would react to her and had to adapt to this. Up until now, she said, she had been able to force things into some sort of shape through incredibly hard work and attention to detail, but now the complexity of what she was dealing with made that impossible. This led her to the conclusion that the statement 'I don't know' is not always a sign of weakness but sometimes could be a sign of strength. This was one of her biggest breakthroughs and took us back to the multiple nuances of grey in the world. After finally reporting on a successful presentation of her new strategy to the board, she admitted: 'I could even get to like the grey,' before adding, 'in moderation, of course!'

The hall of mirrors: Generating uncertainty

Uncertainty is a function of living in an interpersonal world, where we can never definitively know what other people are experiencing or intending. Empathy and other interactional skills can help in this but it is also important to know how much uncertainty you may be transmitting to others, otherwise ambiguity can generate itself like a virus.

This was Ivan's situation, as he tried to adapt to running a marketing team in a new company. He complained that his staff were constantly second-guessing him: trying to out-manoeuvre him, side-step his intentions and deliberately misinterpret what he was saying. The result was that what had seemed, to him, like a relatively routine job was turning into a nightmare. A keen film buff, he said: 'It's like the hall of mirrors in that Orson Welles film, *Lady from Shanghai*. I don't know who is who anymore. And I'm not sure I'm going to survive the shoot-out!'

When we started analysing the incidents of misunderstanding that Ivan was describing it became clear that his vision for running his team was vague and badly defined. The only thing that seemed clear was that this team was very different from the sophisticated, specialized marketing teams Ivan had been used to. It was much more down to earth and practically orientated. I also got the sense that the misunderstandings stemmed less from a deliberate attempt to misinterpret what Ivan was saying but, on the contrary, an eagerness to fill in the gaps that his surprising lack of clarity created. For someone with an illustrious reputation for defining a brand identity, Ivan spoke in staccato sentences and used an arcane vocabulary that I found difficult to decipher at times and could imagine his team did as well. By clarifying his terms and spending more time in one-to-ones and less time grandstanding in guru-like, 'inspirational' talks that he expected his team to turn into specific actions, Ivan started to bring more certainty into the proceedings. At least it began to be clear where people disagreed with him and where they didn't. He, in turn, became more focused on what he really understood about the role and what he didn't. Sometimes, establishing the boundary between the known and the unknown is the most important aspect of managing uncertainty.

Ivan later compared his situation to 'the passing dance', where two people trying to pass in the street both take a step in the same direction, which they then try to correct by both moving in the opposite direction, and so on. The ambiguity in his situation didn't disappear overnight, in part because of the complexity of the brands he was working on, but his management style changed so that he started to generate the certainty that was available rather than proliferating uncertainty.

Ivan's case also flags up the ambiguity that is immanent in language, evidenced by the fact that almost every phrase and word we use can be interpreted in many different ways. The literary theorist William Empson (1930) wrote a famous work entitled *Seven Types of Ambiguity*, studying the deliberate use of multivalent meanings in literature. At times, commercial wordsmiths, such as Ivan, can also use verbal ambiguity to convey their clients' messages. Like the ambiguous figures developed by Gestalt psychologists – for example, the vase that can also be seen as two faces (Spinelli, 1989) – verbal ambiguity aims to open itself up to more than one meaning at a time. In coaching, the key thing is to disentangle deliberate ambiguity from the accidental confusions of imprecise communication. English, with its vast vocabulary and many different dialects, is perhaps more likely to produce ambiguity than some other languages. In the multilingual environment of the contemporary workplace, where for many executives English is not their first language, misunderstandings are rife. Sometimes coaching can act as a kind of textual criticism by simply trying to bring clarity to the usage of language, as well as focusing on the more dramatic issues that a client is compelled to make choices about.

Finding your personal dialectic of uncertainty

Coaching uncertainty is also about helping the client to realize the limits of certainty. Everyone has their personal dialectic, a way in which they most successfully walk the tightrope of uncertainty. Sangita's personal dialectic was always likely to be biased on the side of certainty rather than uncertainty. Others are able to push out towards uncertainty to a much greater extent. In so doing they may well extend their creativity and ability to respond productively to different situations. Fight uncertainty too ferociously, it might be said, and you can defeat yourself.

This is definitely what Chen, a chief executive of a PR agency, discovered. He came to see that uncertainty is present in everything and that the more he could embrace it, the more he could benefit from it, personally and professionally. In our final session together, he said:

> Once I thought I had to come up with answers all the time. It's true you need to assert yourself every now and again, so that the client doesn't think 'I'm doing all the work, so why am I paying him?' But the real stuff, I tend to find these days, is remaining comfortable with the customer's uncertainty for as long as possible. Learning to unlearn is useful – not second-guessing everything, but trying to stay with what clients are telling me and let the answers evolve between us.

This approach didn't mean that Chen neglected his preparations for a client meeting. In fact, he still seemed to prepare quite meticulously and had elaborate back-up plans, which could be used especially for customers who, as he said, 'won't really start thinking about what they want until they've heard a pitch'. But for many clients, especially in open-ended campaigns, Chen's way of using the unknowns in a situation as a potential source of inspiration resulted in much more creative relationships. To be sure, it's not something that works for everybody, as many people require a greater certainty quotient to be able to function at their best. But, as we'll see in Chapter 19, the ability to stay with the uncertainties and ambiguities of the possibilizing stage of the choice cycle is often a crucial factor in producing true creativity.

Part 4

Coaching in the self dimension

10

Coaching final choices and dilemmas

Choice plays a part at every stage of coaching but sometimes a client's difficult decisions and painful dilemmas form the main subject matter of a coaching session or even an entire coaching series. In terms of the Achievement Matrix, this is where we reach Phase 5, when a final strategy needs to be decided on and the coachee may have to go deep into the personal dimension of his being to find the answer.

Coaching final choices is about defining the real choices involved, as 'mirage choices' often obscure the actual issues that have to be resolved. For example, knowing what you have to renounce in a choice can often be more important than knowing what you will gain by it. In this chapter, we also look at risk-managing choice, the effectiveness of formal decision-making tools, 'parallel choice' strategies and some problematic choice-making styles. Finally, we examine choices that have already been made by coachees, albeit unwittingly, a process of revelation that can be frustrating for some and liberating for others.

The leap into the unknown

Let's start by looking at coaching situations where final choices can turn out to be surprisingly straightforward. However much we may try to explore the implications of a significant choice, at its core it remains a leap into the unknown. So simply talking through the choice and, as it were, gazing together into the chasm of uncertainty can itself be immensely clarifying. One effect of this can be to induce the client to choose cautiously, which often turns out to be the optimal choice. For example, Ralph, a media CEO, was, at the last minute, plunged into indecision about a takeover that he had spent a year setting up. Everything was about to be signed and announced to the press, when he suddenly began to doubt whether this was the best way forward for his company. 'It's only when you get to this final stage,' Ralph eventually concluded, 'that you can really look at what an acquisition means. The truth is that this move made great sense a year ago; today it doesn't.' In spite of ruffling many feathers on the boards of both companies, he decided not to go ahead with the takeover.

Sometimes, however, having fully considered his options, the client chooses to move towards increased risk. This can seem to hurl the client towards unrealistic goals but it is often a positive move and even a kind of liberation. Take Emma, whose coaching was focused on her feelings of inadequacy as the manager of a small administrative team. When, much to her astonishment, she was offered a bigger role, running a group ten times the size of her current team, she was naturally inclined to turn it down. Yet as we talked through it, in spite of her negative views, I sensed something new in her tone, a steely determination I had not noticed in her before. Next session she announced she had taken the new job. 'It's the biggest challenge I've ever had but maybe that's what I need. Everything's against it, so why not give it a go!' It turned out to be a success. This kind of situation is very difficult to judge in advance, as sometimes it is the increased effort and concentration involved in contemplating a leap into the unknown that makes the difference. Only once a decision has been made do things really fall into place.

The dialectic of renunciation

If, in coaching, choices sometimes seem to resolve themselves almost by their own volition, at other times they can be much more obdurate. The coaching project may feel like riding a switch-back of indecision or wading through a muddy swamp. In a tough choice, one of the principal factors at play is the dialectic of gain and loss, reward and renunciation. Choice can seem like an expansion, which takes the client into new relationships and new experiences, but it is also a contraction. 'For every yes there must be a no', writes Irvin Yalom (1980: 318). 'To decide one thing always means to relinquish something else.' Affirmation of one course of action involves the negation of another. This can be relatively clear when a choice can be described as 'cutting your losses', when it is obvious that a price has to be paid for the possibility of a gain. In other cases, the opportunity cost of a major decision can be more difficult to assess.

'I'm on the rack. I can't sleep. I can't think about anything except this decision and the more I think about it the less I'm able to deal with it.' These were Dennis's first words to me. His dilemma was whether to swap his role as a middle-manager in a large corporation, with a generous expense account and a good deal of job security, for a much more adventurous and risky role leading a start-up company with a former colleague. He was sleeping badly and was so tied up with his choice that he felt he was paying insufficient attention to his 6-week-old daughter, who, incidentally, was another cause of his sleeplessness.

The choice was particularly difficult because the more we explored Dennis's values and desires, the more it seemed he was inclined to the creativity and adventure of entrepreneurship rather than the more stolid virtues of the corporate life. But what would he be giving up if he took the new role? The prospect of an equity share in the start-up business was tempting but the venture offered no immediate stability and had not even acquired offices. Dennis became increasingly clear that this option would impose too much of a burden on his young family but the thought of relinquishing this opportunity tormented him.

We kept coming back to the cardinal question, what did he really want? In the end, answering this question enabled Dennis to make his final choice and turn down the offer. What he wanted, he concluded, was to be an entrepreneur but what he needed at that moment was to stay in the comparative safety of the corporate world. Whatever he said 'no' to now, he would find a way to say 'yes' to, when the time was right. That was an important insight for Dennis, as I reminded him a few years later when he eventually started his own company.

Encouraging choice-making

One of the biggest factors in choice-making is the perceived risk involved. One way of helping a coachee to manage this risk is to ask him to identify the uniqueness of the dilemma facing him. Is there a chance that the event in question will be repeated or is it a once in a lifetime occurrence? Evidence from social psychology suggests that when the scarcity value of an event is high, its potential persuasiveness increases (Cialdini, 1984). One client who was in property demonstrated this, when he struggled to make up his mind whether to purchase a large country house for redevelopment. 'Something like this comes up very rarely,' he said, 'owned by the same family for hundreds of years . . . unique location.' As a business venture, it seemed there were many less risky projects in his usual territory of up-market town houses but the thought of letting this singular property slip through his fingers was painful and in the end he decided to acquire it.

Sometimes the most effective way of helping a client to break the log jam of a major choice is to encourage them to make smaller choices. As George Eliot wrote in *Daniel Deronda* (1995: 550): 'The strongest principle of growth lies in human choice.' In other words, choosing breeds choosing. The more we make choices, even relatively insignificant ones, the more comfortable we become with the process. By contrast, once a major dilemma sets in, all sorts of choices can get implicated, even though, strictly speaking, they may be unrelated to it. The result can be a growing lack of confidence in the ability to go through the choice cycle at all.

Consider the case of Mal, who for two and a half years had a dilemma hanging over him about whether to merge his team with another department in his TV production company. The decision seemed to drift in and out of his world, with variable urgency, but he was unable to bring it to a resolution. I asked Mal if he could remember a time when he had been able to make significant choices fluently. He said he had always thought of himself as reasonably decisive but in the past he had always felt under pressure from others to make choices quickly and that pressure had now disappeared. 'Perhaps I've just become too much a part of the establishment', he said. Recalling himself at his peak made him realize just how differently he now felt about his work. He said, 'it feels like I'm in a dead zone, where the mobile phone doesn't work'. He decided to get involved in a small work project around diversity. We talked through the stages of the choice cycle it involved, step by step. Transforming his intentions into actions helped him to get back into a more positive frame of mind, as far as choice-making was concerned. As a result, he finally decided not to go ahead with the merger of his team and presented a vigorous business case justifying his strategy.

The lesser evil

On occasion, choices are difficult to make because all the outcomes appear negative. When dusk descends on the choice landscape, picking out marginally brighter colours is not easy. Often the difficulty in seeing the lesser evil is caused by focusing on imaginary, mirage choices rather than the choices that are actually at hand. For example, Craig was so disappointed at having failed to attract either of his preferred candidates for a new IT operation that he found it almost impossible to focus on selecting the candidates who were still available. Focusing on 'the least worst' of these executives slowly helped him to move from the choices that he wasn't in a position to make, to those he was.

Often in these trying conditions, other choices enter the landscape and obscure the original choice. Revealing these can be like unpacking a Russian doll. For instance, in Craig's situation, it was easy to contemplate scrapping the idea of the new operation altogether or changing its funding so as to make it more attractive to the preferred candidates. Of course, this morphing of choices sometimes leads to positive new possibilities but it can also lead to convoluted choices, where the original issue has been overlaid by so many other issues that its meaning has been distorted. Trying to establish the lesser of the two evils involved at least captures the positive and negative dialectic that frames the choice.

This approach certainly seemed to help Paula in her role of integrating two independent law firms following the sudden departure of the partner who had brought about the merger. The senior partners involved in the process seemed intent only on making decisions that directly suited their own interests and ignoring any other decisions. This left Paula dangerously exposed in the middle, potentially being blamed by others for inaction but powerless to act herself. The whole merger was suffused in an emotionally charged atmosphere of nostalgia, doubt, anger and wistful talk about 'the choices that might have been'. But for Paula it was important to cut through the problematic nature of the merger and do the best she possibly could in the situation. She did this largely by focusing on the consequences of not integrating effectively, such as the demoralization of the staff, the loss of reputation and the opportunity created for competitors. ' "Faute de mieux" has become my watchword', she said. Drawing attention to the greater evil of the firm's situation finally helped Paula to define her role and 'persuade other people to make the choices only *they* could make', as she said. In this way, the integration of the firms started in earnest.

Parallel choices

So far we've looked at choices that involve option A or option B, but choices are not always binary; they are sometimes parallel: A *and* B. At best, parallel choices can be sophisticated strategies for achieving goals in uncertain, changing circumstances. Compromise selections can enable you to hedge your bets and lay off risks in a multiple, layered strategy. As long as these duplicate choices are conducted intelligently and in good faith, they can be highly effective responses to complex choice scenarios. For some clients, creating a back-up plan – and even a back-up plan for the back-up plan – is the only way they can ease themselves into a final decision.

But the space between 'yes' and 'no', however alluring, can also be destructive. Sometimes trying to accomplish plans A and B makes it impossible for either to be realized. One client, in attempting to take a restructuring decision that was both strategically progressive and popular with her staff, created a situation in which it was extremely difficult to think through either goal. In the end, she realized she had to prioritize one option or the other. 'The best of both worlds' has a nasty habit of turning into 'the worst of both worlds'. Parallel choice-making can also encourage political one-upmanship, as Chris Argyris (1966) suggests, where choices are motivated less by a desire to find the best possible option as to be seen to do the right thing or gain advantages over rivals. One client, faced with a difficult strategic decision, revealed that his real concern was not losing face in front of his board, so he developed a hugely complex proposal that seemed to cater for every eventuality but that he knew could never be implemented.

In fact, compromise strategies are often a mask for an evasion of choice. Duplicating options in this way can amount to following the line of least resistance when in reality a much tougher choice is called for. Bad faith of this sort is a form of unconscious self-deception, even though we often have no way of avoiding it. At a conscious level, the challenge in a compromise plan is judging exactly when to react to the built-in triggers of action. But if a person moves from plan A to plan B at the first sign of difficulty, this may play to their weaknesses in choice-making and suggest that a single option might have been the more productive strategy.

Something like this occurred with Katie, a lobbyist, who was determined to confront a difficult customer whom she was 'over-servicing', that is, providing too much of her time for the fee that had been agreed. The client could be charming but in the past had become aggressive when fees were mentioned and threatened to move his contract to another agency. Katie decided against an all-or-nothing strategy. 'If I do that I'm worried I'll chicken out and keep things as they are', she explained. So she settled for a compromise strategy, raising the rates for the frontline services she was providing but offering the customer an attractive discount on a secondary offering.

When she met the client, Katie introduced the discount on the secondary service in glowing terms, 'in order to sweeten the pill'. The client greeted this proposal enthusiastically and started talking in encouraging terms about how he might extend his business with the agency. Too late, Kate realized that the client appeared to think he was being offered a discount on all the company's services! Paralysed by this realization, Katie was unable to even challenge her client's (perhaps deliberate) misunderstanding of her offer. It was only after several sessions of soul-searching that Katie decided that she could not afford a compromise approach. Her sole priority had to be to communicate the price rise, which she finally did at a subsequent client meeting. Sometimes, it seems, our choices are indeed binary – all or nothing.

Problematic choice-making styles

Let's now look at some other potentially problematic ways of making choices that may emerge in coaching. One common way of making executive decisions is to delegate them to others. In the short term, this can be an effective way of 'solving' choices and, as a democratic management style, can be positive in empowering a team. But this style can cause difficulties when the buck really does stop with you and a major choice needs to be made. This, at least, was what George discovered. He had come to rely totally on his boss, Jan, to make all his decisions. Jan had realized this and was determined to force George to make the decisions he had been hired to make. An elaborate cat and mouse game then ensued, with George desperately trying to get Jan to indicate her preferences on key business areas, so that he would avoid confrontation with her or the consequences of making the wrong choices. This game of 'choice tag' consisted of writing policy papers for Jan to agree or disagree with or trying to lure Jan into declaring her hand by subtly introducing searching questions into a discussion of another subject. George also spent a good deal of time talking to

Jan's personal assistant, 'trying to find out the lie of the land'. Ultimately, by analysing these actions in coaching, George began to realize the exhausting futility of this approach and summoned up the courage to start making choices on his own.

Delegated decisions fall into the category of what the pioneering psychologist William James (1890: 532) classified as choices, in which we let ourselves 'drift with a certain indifferent acquiescence in a direction accidentally determined from without'. These drifting choices are subtly left to some external agency to make, whether it is a person, group, unexpected occurrence or just the flow of events. An effort may be made to make a choice, but deep down the executive is simply waiting for someone – or something – to make the decision for him.

The opposite problem is overpersonalizing decisions. This may arise when an executive takes an exceptionally high degree of personal responsibility for issues that others might regard as the province of external forces, such as the senior management of an organization or society in general. This way of thinking can be admirable, even heroic, but it can also confuse the personal and interpersonal dimensions of an issue in a way that conceals the real choices involved. For example, Claudio, a banker, wrestled with his conscience about the amount of remuneration he was receiving, following an extended stay in West Africa. He began to complain about being overpaid and sought to influence the bank's remuneration policy, starting with that of his own team. The more he discussed the issue, however, the more he concluded that the high level of remuneration 'came with the territory' and was what attracted many people to the industry in the first place. He realized that his real choice was whether to continue in banking or not, a dilemma that he eventually resolved by leaving the profession.

Personality biases are also closely connected to choice-making styles and often have a bearing on final choices. For example, clients who are originators may find it easy to deal with choices at an abstract level but more difficult to come to final conclusions at the probabilizing stage. This may be because they find detailed choice-making unstimulating, preferring to move on to the next intellectual challenge, or because at this stage there is a whole range of practical choices to make that may challenge their bold ideas. By contrast, accommodators are likely to excel at the 'nuts and bolts' choices that enable a project to be completed but may be much more perplexed by choices that involve major change. For example, one client who was required to re-engineer his entire department, as the result of a takeover, spent a whole session going through the history of the department in great detail before he was ready to even start considering whether or not he should comply with the new management's demands.

Traditional decision-making tools

What about formal decision-making tools – can these help to resolve difficult choices in coaching? A basic strategic tool, such as cost–benefit analysis, can certainly help some clients to work through the pros and cons of a decision and to identify the values and implications embedded in each option. In effect, this tool is simply another form of oppositional enquiry. However, when we come to more elaborate methods, in my view, we run up against the tendency for excessive rationalism of most decision-making theories. A 'rational' model, such as 'the even-swap method' (Hammond et al., 1989), presents choice as a series of carefully selected options that need to be weighted according to their merits. This may be useful at the probabilizing stage of the choice cycle but the model assumes that the possibilizing stage is unproblematic, when in fact many people find it extremely challenging, even trying to avoid it altogether, for fear of opening up a Pandora's Box of choice. Without optimal options, there can be no optimal selection. Rationalistic models also tend to ignore the implementation stage of the choice cycle, as though making the right selection were tantamount to putting it into practice; yet it is only in action that we can really assess the validity of a choice.

Rationalistic approaches to decision-making can also present a false impression of choice in that they are too reliant on examples of choices, which are more simplistic than are likely to occur in reality. They often imply an apparently complete knowledge of past events, which fails to do justice to the lived experience of choice-making. Retrospectively, we have the luxury of omniscience, knowing much more than could be known at the time, but this distorts the amount of certainty ever available in the present. So it is important to help the coachee to analyse past decisions not only retrospectively but also prospectively, as they were made, in terms of a complex, only partially knowable present, facing an unknown future. As Kierkegaard (1996: 61) said: 'life must be understood backwards . . . [but] it must be lived forwards'.

Nevertheless, decision-making tools can work for some clients. For very rationally orientated clients, a meticulous arrangement of pros and cons is often reassuring and productive. Assessing the level of risk in an option and even assigning probability in percentages may help some clients to 'think themselves' into a decision. For other clients, this kind of procedure may be a waste of time. For emotionally inclined clients, for instance, it is unlikely that purely rational criteria will ever be binding, because feelings can create quite a different loading of factors in a decision. One client said that in recruitment interviews, he was always led by 'gut feeling', rather than the candidates' experience or qualifications. He made recruitment decisions entirely on his 'intuitive sense' of how a person would fit in with his team.

The impasse or holding pattern

Is there always a resolution for final choices and dilemmas? Sometimes the answer is 'no', at least not in the form the client may have been expecting. Instead of a dramatic change the client may seem to end up in an impasse. This may be experienced as frustrating but often it is a specific form of waiting rather than a total dead end, rather like the holding pattern in which an airline pilot flies as he awaits clearance to land. The client is often in a perfect balance between interacting forces, which prevents any significant immediate change. Inertia may seem to be the winner here and yet, through this delicate interplay of interactions, a new appreciation of oneself and one's situation may emerge.

This was the experience of Sylviane, a manager in a market research company. She entered coaching because of 'nagging doubts about her role'. She said that she had 'a tremendous need for some kind of change' but wasn't clear what it was. As we explored her situation, it became apparent that her managing director had prevented her from making changes to the way her team was structured and its range of activities. This frustrated her but when she thought of leaving the company she found that any advantage in doing so was matched by an equally strong reason to stay: weight and counterweight were in complete equivalence. This seemed to be partially due to personality factors. She was personally ambitious but very team-orientated; she wanted to confront her boss, yet owed him a great debt of loyalty. Other roles she looked at within the same group of companies seemed to offer a different set of neutralizing balances: too much responsibility or too little, more travel but less job security, and so on. In the end, she concluded that she was where she wanted to be, at least for the time being. 'The nagging doubt is still there, from time to time,' she said, 'but it doesn't really bother me any more. I feel I'm in a good job with good people. If something better comes along, I'll know it when I see it.'

Already-made choices: The case of Ronnie T.

Some coaching resolutions that may superficially resemble an impasse are actually a kind of liberation for the client. This is because as human beings we cannot avoid making choices and sometimes the choices we agonize over we have in fact already made, although we don't fully realize it. By a neat twist of oppositional logic, what seemed to be the problem turns out to be the solution. Bringing these 'already-made choices' to the surface can provide some of the surprises that make coaching so rewarding, for both coachee and coach.

Ronnie T. is a case in point. He was a senior executive in a large retail organization who had worked his way up from store manager to regional manager and a series of corporate roles. A tall New Zealander, with a deadpan sense of humour, he was now a senior advisor in the operations department but he felt he had hit a dead end in his career. Everyone around him seemed younger than him and his boss gave no indication that he was ever likely to vacate his role. He saw himself slowly slipping down the hierarchy and 'being stuck' in support roles for the rest of his career. 'I don't want a walk-on part,' he said, 'I want another starring role, at least, for one last time.'

Ronnie talked a lot about his leadership abilities and his experience in 'taking charge of situations and making things happen', but most of his stories about his career seemed to be about the satisfaction he got from helping people. We looked at his ISO profile and he came out as an accommodator rather than an originator. This surprised him since innovation had been a hallmark of his most successful roles, including devising a new distribution scheme for his region, which had earned him the attention of head office. When we analysed this project, it turned out that his scheme was very much a practical response to a particular set of difficulties rather than innovation for its own sake.

When I asked Ronnie about the leaders he admired in the company, he mentioned Clayton, the marketing director. 'I can't help feeling that someone like Clayton has got it all', Ronnie said. 'I'm tagging along, fixing up bits and pieces, advising on training or helping people with strategies.' I asked him what it was that most appealed to him in Clayton and his role. 'Everyone knows that the business revolves around marketing, doesn't it?' He said this in a rather flat tone (even by his deadpan standards) and then tailed off. I asked him: 'Is that what is really important to you, the status of the job?' He looked troubled, although all he said was, 'Good question!', and at that point we had to end the session.

It was several weeks before I saw Ronnie again but the moment he walked into the room I noticed a new spring in his lengthy stride. He looked invigorated, alert, 10 years younger in fact. I suspected he had been offered a new job but luckily I bracketed this thought and refrained from voicing it. Ronnie started by saying: 'I've finally figured out that I am where I need to be. I am who I am.' He said he had realized that much of what he professed to think about leadership was more about what others believed rather than his own feelings. The same was true about the hierarchy of roles within the organization. 'There's tons of talk by people that support roles are just a cost to the business but support roles are not a cost. Without us there is no business.'

Ronnie found it hard to put his finger on exactly what had made him change his mind. At first he thought he was just giving up and settling for the easy life, but gradually he realized he was finally accepting what he really wanted. Helping others gave him more satisfaction than he had credited. He said he had found himself thinking more and more about the time his son had spent in hospital a year earlier, following a minor road accident. 'It opens your eyes to what's important, that kind of thing', he said. 'In that environment, it's all about support and care, not who's got the biggest ego.' Whatever had brought about this change of heart, it proved to be profound and Ronnie was genuinely renewed by it, as an executive and as a person.

11

Coaching confidence

Choosing confidence?

Self-confidence is at the heart of how we feel about ourselves and our ability to achieve what we want. It can be the most mercurial of qualities, arbitrating between high performance and abject failure, as many sportsmen and women have discovered. Issues around self-confidence occur frequently in coaching, as it influences many of the ways in which we make choices, and coaching seems to help. In fact, in my experience, improved self-confidence is one of the benefits that executives are most likely to attribute to coaching. For that reason alone, it merits a separate chapter.

Can clients choose confidence or does confidence choose them? Some clients think the latter. For them, confidence is a matter of biology, upbringing or luck. 'It's like I'm guilty until proved innocent,' one client said, 'I start off thinking I can't do it, and then sometimes I'm proved wrong!' But coaching can help to make the client realize just how much difference he can make to his own levels of confidence.

So how do you coach for confidence? In this chapter, we look at the lived experience of confidence and identify the crucial role that the future plays in it. Understanding a client's self-dialogue around confidence is also important, as is distinguishing confidence from competence. Confidence can manifest itself in a relentless personal dialectic of confidence and doubt, which can make effective choice-making extremely challenging, as we'll see in returning to the case of Gerry O., introduced in Chapter 1. At the same time, we'll explore how a coach working oppositionally can actually help a client to use her self-doubt as a means of developing self-confidence.

The dialectic of 'can' and 'can't'

What is the phenomenology of confidence? Ask coachees to describe the experience of feeling confident and the phrases that occur often include the following:

> I feel I am able to achieve what I am intending. . . . I feel sure that I can cope with whatever is thrown at me. . . . I know I can put all the doubts aside and come through. . . . I know I can do it.

Statements like these reveal one thing immediately: confidence relates to the future. Time plays a crucial role in the phenomenon of self-confidence. It is an anticipation of future events in the form of a conviction that things will turn out well. This is not necessarily a blind faith in the future but an assurance that if things go wrong you have the personal and social resources to put them right.

What these statements also reveal is the importance of the phrase 'I can'. The dialectic of self-confidence and self-doubt is in part an interaction between 'can do' and 'can't do', and it's one that we all experience. It's not that confident people have no doubts, it's just that they are usually better at overcoming those doubts than people who lack confidence. Making choices around this dialectic is crucial. When confidence breaks down, doubt can come in the form of a severance of the future from the past. So reminding a client of past successes, even if they are not strictly related to the project in hand, can be productive. 'When you think of past success what do you feel?', I asked a client, who had lost all faith in her ability to run her team. 'Good, of course,' she replied, 'you get a surge of enthusiasm. It's a bit like that moment when a plane takes off.' When I asked her to identify the principal sentence she had in her head at that point she said: 'I guess it's that tough things can be conquered, I can do it if I have to.'

Sometimes helping the client to identify such 'can do moments' and turn them into a personal imperative has a positive effect. Perhaps combined with visualization this can become a tool for managing confidence. Recognizing this kind of experience – what another client, Gwyneth, called her 'ashes and sackcloth moments' – is itself extremely valuable. This type of self-reflection is an instance of super-reflection, as if the individual is both in the experience and able to recognize it from without.

The real danger of the 'can't do' attitude is that what is essentially a temporary vision of the future becomes permanent. Once this interpretation settles to a level of pre-reflective assumptions, it manifests itself in such beliefs as: 'I will never do anything positive. . . . Things always turn out badly for me. . . . I am not the sort of person who accomplishes difficult tasks.' This is a pattern of choices that can be hard to change. It may even be the case that the client is unconsciously choosing defeat, not simply in his overall attitude to future events but in his premature reactions to anything that seems to confirm that things are turning against him. This hyper-vigilance for such turning points often converts mildly negative or even neutral events into harbingers of doom, which seem to confirm the inevitability of defeat. This becomes a self-fulfilling prophecy as this pattern of choices generalizes itself to others. Organizationally, the diminution of confidence can be contagious, a self-generating spiral in which an executive loses some of his self-confidence, causing others to start to lose confidence in him, which increases his own self-doubts, and so on.

Expert listening can break this pattern. In the coach, the coachee encounters someone who has acquired a certain immunity from the contagion of lost confidence. The coach's readiness to listen to the client's story without prejudice can itself help the coachee to reinterpret the negative spiral of choices in which she is involved. Openly enquiring into the causes of the client's self-doubts and clarifying some of her assumptions about their meaning can also help to open up new possibilities. In this way, the twisting tornado of doubt, which may sweep away a client's self-confidence, can be set on a different course.

Asking the cardinal questions and going through stages of the choice cycle can also help to establish a new pattern of choosing. Often after a major setback the client simply needs to work through an achievement process that may have become so disrupted that choices that were taken for granted now seem to be hazardous and uncertain. Helping the client 'get back in the saddle' by deconstructing a failed task and then going through the process of planning a new one can often restore lost confidence. At best, it creates a new awareness of the skills necessary to accomplish a task, which can lead to improved performance.

The self-dialogue of confidence

What happens to a client's self-dialogue when his confidences rises or falls? This can be an important question for the coach to help to answer. For example, here is Peter, a sales executive, talking eloquently about a recent tennis game:

> I'm serving for the set; I know I can do it. My opponent returns with a tremendous backhand (and I'm thinking, 'where did that come from?'), followed by a weak volley into the net by myself ('typical!'). The pressure of winning starts to impinge on me. I begin to think: 'I never beat him, I was up like this in my first set and it came to nothing.' My hand shakes slightly, I throw the ball too high and my serve action is jerky. Result – double fault and my mindset changes. I'm thinking, 'this has gone, it's hopeless' and the match just seems to dissolve.

Images of the future abound here and in a sense what is happening is that Peter is already in the future while the present is still occurring. This lightening-fast excursion into the future is a kind of mental time travel. It could be useful were it not so steeped in negativity, for the future that is experienced is essentially a future of defeat, which is why cognitive therapist Aron Beck (1976) called this tendency 'catastrophizing'.

    'Storyboarding' is a technique that enables us to visualize this almost Hogarthian cartoon of change, in which the images change from the positive to the worried, from the harassed to the miserable, before ending up in downright ruination. It is a storyboard, complete with lines, images and feeling. Understanding this mental and emotional script and describing each image in the sequence can help the client to understand that he is in many ways writing this story himself, which can of course help him to rewrite it. A positive storyboard, with strong value lines, such as 'I can do it', often restores hope and keeps the client focused on the present. The effect is to focus on the process rather than the result. Once Peter started to convince himself that his main task was to play as well as possible, regardless of the result, he stopped channelling all his mental energy into anticipating future defeat – or indeed future victory, which can often be just as destructive.

As the reader may have guessed, improving Peter's tennis game was not the principal aim of his coaching but it seemed to relate so directly to his loss of confidence in his sales ability that it had to be explored. In fact, he had gone through a familiar pattern with successful salespeople: a string of successes for several years and then, for the first time, a sustained period during which he seemed unable to clinch a significant deal. 'I'm devastated, gutted,' he had said in our first session, 'it's affecting my health, my home life, everything.' But looking at his self-dialogue and the kind of catastrophic scripts he was writing himself in sales situations helped to restore some of his confidence. Too often he was either trying to conclude a sale too early in the sales process or failing to properly close the deal for fear of rejection. He was doing this in rather subtle and unusual ways but once he began to identify these tendencies his confidence in his sales performance gradually recovered and the results soon followed.

Part of Peter's problem was the way he attributed his lack of success to outside agencies. 'It's how it goes,' he said at first, 'sometimes people lose it and they never get it back. It's just the luck of the draw.' This fatalistic interpretation clearly didn't offer him much prospect of hope, as it placed excessive weight on the negative side of the dialectic of confidence. Looking at attributions like this is always useful. Clients who account for their lack of confidence by saying 'I'm too young' or 'I haven't been trained in that area' or 'my face just doesn't fit' may be highlighting something important or they may be concealing the real reasons for their lack of confidence in such a way that it makes it difficult for them to be addressed.

Confidence or competence?

'Everything connects', wrote the novelist E.M. Forster (1910), and this is certainly true of self-confidence. If a client is to change his choices around confidence he often has to change his choices around other things that he may feel are quite unconnected. For example, Gwyneth, referred to above, was only able to take control of her loss of confidence after a series of setbacks by radically changing her work pattern – and to some extent her lifestyle. She had to be prepared to take more time for calm reflection, rather than live in a whirlwind of meetings, before things could really change for her.

One connection that often needs to be clarified is the interaction between confidence and competence. What may be interpreted by the client as a deep-seated personality issue is sometimes revealed as a more malleable lack of knowledge about how to perform a set of tasks. This can often be identified by retrospective or anticipatory analysis of a task. For instance, George, an administrator who wanted to move into a fund-raising role, became demoralized by his ineffectual efforts at approaching potential donors. 'I'm just not cut out for this kind of thing', he concluded gloomily. But once we analysed his haphazard strategy and his tendency in meetings 'to play it by ear', which probably played to his weakness as a rather intense introvert, it became clear that he was going about his project ineffi-ciently. Once George started using his strengths as a planner to prepare for conversations and meetings – as well as getting the right support from others – he began to develop his own highly effective way of engaging with donors. What he had attributed to 'can't do' turned out to be a case of 'don't know how to do'.

The case of Gerry O. and the rollercoaster of confidence (continued from Chapter 1)

In some cases, the confidence of a client is embedded in a more complex set of interactions between values and desires that are rooted in long-term experiences. For such clients, an intense, often painful, dialectic between 'can do' and 'can't do' becomes a leading force in their life. This was the situation with Gerry O., a senior executive with an international consultancy, whom we met at the beginning of the book. I was asked to spend some sessions with him, in order to give him a chance to assess his future plans for his career. He was charming and polite, with a soft West of Ireland brogue that 30 years of life in London had not erased. We met in an airy meeting room overlooking St Paul's Cathedral, where our session would begin with Gerry pouring us both a cup of tea.

As Gerry went through his life and work narrative, it seemed that he had been very successful but it gradually became apparent that he was discontented with his role in an organization to which he had devoted his entire career. He felt that he had been overlooked for promotions in the previous decade after a meteoric early rise. 'It's not exactly a case of "up like a rocket, down like a stick" but I feel I've been drifting downwards for quite some time', he smiled sadly. It had taken him most of the session to express anything that could be constituted as a criticism of his firm and even now he tried to retract the statement as a self-criticism.

Gerry's main concern was that his real contribution to the firm was not acknowledged. He said that he was under-resourced, having no team of his own, and that others took some of the credit for his work, including his boss, who was based in Tokyo. Rather than wanting to discuss how to smoothly play out his final years at the company, it seemed to me that Gerry wanted his coaching to help him restore justice to his situation. He said that his people-orientated style of management was unappreciated, which made him feel that it was in the interests of others in the company, as well as his own, that he should 'make a stand'. Where he had started the session in somnolent ease, it ended in a mood of almost righteous anger and a fierce determination to confront what he felt was a decade of neglect. He said he was going to work on a strategy to confront his boss and enlist support from his colleagues.

In our second session two weeks later, I was therefore somewhat taken aback when Gerry started by apologizing for the previous session. 'I embarrassed myself. You must think I'm a fool. I don't know why I was so disloyal to the firm. It was just childish.' When I questioned him on his thinking here, the session began to follow the same pattern as the first. Gerry went from smooth denial and self-reproach to irritation, anger and a resolution 'to do something' about the way he was being treated by the company. Come the next session, he was back to charming apology, self-reproach and mild denial, as though the previous meeting had been a dream, before gradually adopting the same tone of resentment and accusation with which he seemed to conclude a session.

Towards the end of the third session of this strange spiralling movement, I began to feel that something more radical was needed to help Gerry make the choices that were right for him. Perhaps the coaching itself was a mistake. But I also wondered if this to-ing and fro-ing between confidence and self-doubt was typical of Gerry's life. 'It seems you are giving me quite an insight into what it's like being you', I said. He looked surprised and then nodded slowly. 'It can be a bit of an inner roller coaster. I can deal with it by psyching myself up and being extremely positive but sooner or later it breaks down.'

At the beginning of our next session, Gerry finally broke the spell. He smiled at me as he put a spoonful of sugar in his tea, 'I'm sorry for playing silly buggers. I now know what I want to do. I can't keep putting myself down forever.' After that the coaching advanced in a much more focused way, as Gerry went about his task of gaining the recognition he deserved with extraordinary resolution. In the end, he secured a team for himself and official designation as leader of the European group.

Gerry had experienced considerable pain in the early part of the coaching but the process of going through the choice cycle in the sessions had brought out into the open what he had silently experienced for years. Helped by his realization that achieving justice for himself set a good example for others in the firm, he was finally able to overcome his self-doubt and redefine his choices accordingly.

The opposite of confidence

In part, Gerry's is a story of opposites and the oppositional dynamics of confidence are always worth considering, for self-doubt is far from being a wholly negative attribute. Indeed, Kierkegaard (2000: 136) spoke of 'the grandeur of doubt' and called it 'the beginning of the highest form of existence, because it can have everything else as its presupposition'. What he meant, I think, is that nothing is sacred, as far as the questioning impetus of doubt is concerned; everything is open to enquiry. Consequently, self-doubting people often have great insight into themselves and they can see aspects of the world that others cannot see.

Interestingly enough, exploring the oppositional logic of confidence with a client often reveals the characteristic in a negative light. For one client, for instance, 'confidence' meant being 'smug and complacent', so why would he want to give up his tendency to doubt himself and everything around him? For another client, 'confidence' was indistinguishable from 'arrogance'; he saw it as a completely unwarranted sense of being able to do anything and talk over anybody who opposes you. Perhaps the truth of arrogance is that it is an attempt to create a confidence that is in reality absent. One client who was widely regarded as the epitome of arrogance by others revealed that his stance was an extreme attempt to rid himself of the self-doubt he constantly experienced. Moving towards a less precarious and more sustainable personal dialectic meant finding aspects of himself that he could authentically believe in.

Exploring the other side of confidence certainly helped Hattie to see herself quite differently. She was an editor in an online information service, who was regarded by her boss as talented and dedicated but lacking the confidence to do justice to herself when dealing with colleagues. 'What does diffidence give you,' I asked her in our second session together, 'what do you get out of it?' She looked a little surprised at my questions but replied: 'Actually, I'm nicer, more authentic, more caring and more right than people who ooze with confidence.' By talking through what she found attractive about her style of being in the world, she became more accepting, and even proud, of her diffidence. She said that people always accused her of being 'reserved', as though it was a vice and not a virtue. Paradoxically, the more confident she became in her diffidence, so to speak, the more open she became to exploring less self-doubting ways of behaving.

A simple exercise helped to move forward this process. 'How would you sit in a meeting if you lacked confidence?', I asked her. She slowly leant back in her seat and slumped her shoulders, making herself look smaller, and frowned slightly. 'Now how would you sit if you were confident?', I asked her. A shade more reluctantly, she sat up straighter in her chair, leaned forward across the desk, smiled a little and nodded her head as though following the conversation approvingly. When she analysed which felt best, she was surprised at how much energy the confident gestures and posture gave her. 'There's something in both of them,' she concluded, 'the droopy style is probably more me, but the confident style definitely gives me a lift.' After this, Hattie began to experiment with diffident and confident ways of communicating in meetings. In this way, she discovered her own personal dialectic of confidence, using her own values to develop the style of behaviour that served her best in her professional role.

12

Coaching action and inaction

'There is no reality except in action', says Sartre (1948: 404), and ultimately achievement is about implementation. Only in action can we really know the true status of the desires and the choices we have committed to. Action is the third stage in the choice cycle, and for some clients getting to this stage is a kind of achievement in itself: they have turned long-held dreams or aspirations into tangible plans. Now it is a question of putting their choices into practice, but implementation is itself a field of choice, presenting countless occasions to confirm, modify or even abandon a selected strategy.

As we'll see in this chapter, coaching action is about helping the coachee to maintain her action focus: the right state of mind to implement her choices. Action focus is about finding the appropriate conditions to use one's willpower and overcome possible blocks to achievement, such as half-heartedness, psychological paralysis and panic, in which freedom of choice is experienced as a problem. We also examine the opposite problem, the impulse to rush to action, which can also act as a barrier to effective implementation.

Action focus

Once a decision has been made, psychologists have noticed an interesting phenomenon. We seem to close down our options and become resistant to any suggestion that we have chosen wrongly or that other alternatives have any merit. This cognitive 'confirmation bias' (Wason, 1960) has potential dangers, of course, but one obvious advantage is that it makes it easier for us to implement our choices. This closing down movement, so different to the opening up process of the first stage of the choice cycle, is exactly what is necessary to put an action plan into practice. Rather than having to re-choose again and again, we can commit ourselves to practical achievement.

Yet it can be surprising just how quickly some clients are inclined to veer from their chosen objectives. The desire to improvise can be perplexingly strong in some people, perhaps because it is experienced as a relief from the stress that can occur when anticipating action. It is likely to be more pronounced for clients who prefer spontaneity rather than planning. Although this openness and flexibility may be an advantage in action situations, it can mean risking all the good work that has gone into the early stages of the choice cycle.

Consider this incident, related to me by Phillip, a managing director, who was on the point of delivering a speech to the entire staff of his media-buying company. It was a major strategic presentation that he had worked on with his board and the communications teams for the best part of six weeks. They had improved the text many times, looking at every angle of the new strategy, and had fully rehearsed the talk to general approbation:

> About five minutes before I was due to go on, I was overcome by an overwhelming urge to ditch the speech and improvise, something I've never been particularly good at, I have to say. I don't know why. I was feeling quite nervous and I had the script in my hand but it felt like a lead weight that I had to get rid of. I went over to Jamie, our communications director, and whispered to him: 'Do you think I should just go with the flow?' I'll never forget the look of horror on his face. 'No,' was all he said, 'stick to what we've prepared.' He was absolutely right, of course.

This is where the value of monitoring goals in coaching comes in. Just as establishing the client's vision and setting objectives can be surprisingly useful activities in themselves, so monitoring goal achievement can help the client to assess the quality of his attempts at change. Monitoring also has a quantitative aspect, as it is easy to underestimate how often an action may have to be performed in order to be successful. As already suggested, repetition is a temporal virtue that is not always appreciated. Clients often think that by doing something once they have done enough to cement long-lasting change. There is a parallel here with organizational change programmes, which, according to leadership theorist John Kotter (1996), frequently fail, in part because companies underestimate how often certain actions, such as communicating strategy, will need to be repeated. Likewise, in individual change programmes, it is sometimes necessary for the coachee to appreciate the unspectacular but effective virtues of perseverance.

Willpower

Another way of understanding this whole-hearted and 'whole-headed' commitment to action, which we call action focus, is through the notion of willpower. This concept has had a slightly dubious reputation in the past, perhaps through its association with an inauthentic idea of 'duty', as something that one forces oneself to perform against one's wishes. But willpower can in fact be seen as a very pure expression of what we want to do, a positive and purposeful orientation towards the future that enables us to engage in action freely. In relation to existential psychotherapy, Yalom (1980: 339) has said that 'The therapist's task is to disencumber will' and the same might be said of interactional coaching, especially when it comes to the action stage of the choice cycle.

Interestingly, if we look at the Latin root of the word 'volition', which is a synonym for 'will', we find that it also means 'to wish' or 'to want'. Willpower seems to express itself most fluently where there is harmony between the client's desires and his actions. As such, it is a compelling personal resource, which Rollo May (1969: 218) describes in the following terms, using the word 'wish' instead of 'desire':

'Wish' gives the warmth, the content, the imagination, the child's play, the freshness, and the richness to 'will'. 'Will' gives the self-direction, the maturity to 'wish'. Without 'wish' 'will' loses its life-blood, its viability, and tends to expire in self-contradiction. If you only have 'will' and no 'wish' you have the dried up, Victorian, neopuritan man.

When this fusion of wishing and willing occurs, coaching can largely focus on monitoring actions, reacting to setbacks and encouraging, challenging and looking out for new goals. This can be an exhilarating and rewarding experience all around. However, achieving this balance is not easy. Just as behind the apparently effortless poise of a ballet dancer or surf-boarder there is a complex, ongoing synthesis of choices, so in the executive world real achievement involves a delicate balance of interactions that can be disrupted all too easily.

Coaching inaction

How do we coach clients when an obstacle arises between their chosen action and its implementation? Instead of freedom we now have unfreedom. This may manifest itself as an apparently half-hearted approach to action on the part of the coachee: a crab-like sideways approach to a challenge, picking off some tasks but holding back on the more difficult ones. This mood bears similarities to what Heidegger (1962: 240) calls 'hankering after possibilities', which in reality 'closes off the possibilities'. Of course, this may be a client's way of working up momentum or waiting for the right oppor-tunity to act. But the difference between moving slowly and stopping altogether can sometimes be a thin one, especially if the client begins to feel there is more road ahead than road behind, so to speak. So it is important to understand if this half-heartedness is prompted by excessive cautiousness or genuine doubt about a course of action.

Paralysis

Two more extreme impediments to action are psychological paralysis and panic. These situations are quite distinct from the dilemmas we looked at in Chapter 10, which involve hesitation in making a decision. In the case of these blockages, the decision seems to have been made; the problem is implementing it.

Psychological paralysis is a feeling of being unable to act, as though an unseen force is holding one back. Sometimes this can be a temporary state and going through the client's action plan may be enough to reassure him of the need to act. But when the mood seems more permanent, the coach needs to help the client to identify what is going on. The client wants to perform the actions but what does she *not* want? Why is she choosing to act as she does, however unconsciously? Fear of criticism or ridicule may be a factor, or concerns about the sheer amount of effort involved in the action. Fear of being out of control can also be an obstacle, especially for executives who are used to a high degree of control at work. One client, who seemed to be unable to put her plans into practice, said to me: 'At least when I'm getting it wrong, I know what I'm doing!' Change itself may be daunting, evoking uncertainty about going into the unknown and becoming a different person. Whatever is holding back the client is not necessarily 'irrational' but discovering its particular and perplexing rationality can be a challenge.

At this point, the whole spectrum of coaching approaches and techniques can open up to the interactional coach. For example, oppositional enquiry can identify the other side of the coin: the consequences of not achieving a goal or of not even making an effort. The possibility of a lost opportunity can be a genuine spur to action. Perhaps the coaching itself offers a unique platform for action that the client would prefer not to waste. Or a positive, highly reassuring stance may be effective, in which the coach simply asserts his belief that the client can achieve what he wants, if this is what the coach genuinely believes. Other possibilities for bridging the gulf between intention and reality are helping the client to visualize the desired action or helping him to develop a mantra for the silent repetition of the agreed choices.

Cognitive-behavioural therapeutic techniques, such as thought-stopping (Lazarus, 1981), can sometimes work in these situations but, in my experience, only if the client is willing to take responsibility for his actions, rather than because he is being reconditioned without his conscious awareness, as traditional behaviourists would argue. Techniques are often successful precisely because they enable the client to become aware of the choices they are habitually making and to change them. For example, Molly, an oil company executive, requested anger management tools to help her manage her outbursts of vicious criticism of her colleagues. But when we reviewed her use of these tools, it was plain that she had not made any effort to change her behaviour, rather she simply used them to reinforce her contention that she had no understanding of why she criticized others. 'I don't know why it happens, any more than you do', she told me. Only when she was able to take ownership of the complex thoughts and feelings that motivated her could she begin to control her anger.

One strong source of psychological paralysis is a fear of failure. Life is a constant interaction between success and failure, trial and error, but even the most consistent achievers can become so fixated on failure that success becomes impossible. For example, Edward was a successful painter who periodically suffered from 'artist's block', which often struck when he had a major exhibition coming up. The more enthusiastic he was about his planned paintings, the more likely he was to get blocked. He had tried 'all the tricks of the trade', he said, meditation, chanting, using the clock for very short, 10-minute sessions, but nothing seemed to work. He remained blocked.

We tried to identify what was haunting him. The prospect of others seeing his work seemed to intensify his anxiety. 'It's not just me and the canvas: there is someone looking over my shoulder,' he said, 'someone who in the end will decide to buy it or not.' Although this sense of being overlooked was initially troubling, it seemed to be the fear of not living up to his own expectations that was most powerful. He said that, at his best, his painting was completely spontaneous, as though the brush were making all the decisions. This remark reminded me of Merleau-Ponty's description of a slow-motion film of Henri Matisse in the act of painting. In real-time, the philosopher writes, Matisse's brush seemed bold and decisive, but in slow motion:

> . . . [it] was seen to mediate in a solemn and expanding time . . . to try ten possible movements, dance in front of the camera, brush it lightly several times, and crash down like a lightning stroke upon the one line necessary. (Merleau-Ponty, 1974: 42)

It was as if Edward was endlessly analysing the countless micro-choices he had yet to make on the canvas. So, using oppositional logic, I suggested that instead of producing the best possible painting, he should try to do his worst. 'Just do your worst,' I said, 'and see what happens.' This suggestion amused him greatly but when he tried it, it seemed to free him of overanalysing and got him using his paints again. Although to begin with, he said, he was 'remarkably successful' in achieving his goal of a very bad painting, he soon found himself being drawn into his project 'by an invisible thread'. After a couple of days of this, he was back into his normal state of spontaneous but purposeful creativity, in which his brush led his work rather than his anxiety.

Panic: The ground rush phenomenon

In psychological paralysis it seems that the client's freedom to act has been taken away from him, whereas with the second major type of blockage, panic, it is acting with conscious control that becomes the problem. In a state of panic, action seems to turn into the opposite of what you expected. Instead of experiencing freedom as a positive, it turns into a negative, as your plans unravel in a chaos of seemingly random choices.

The metaphor of 'ground rush' sometimes helps clients to get a different perspective on panic. 'Ground rush' refers to a phenomenon that occurs as a parachutist approaches landing. On the way down, he often experiences very little sensation of falling. The descent is so gradual that the ground seems quite static, with the countryside beautifully laid out, the fields neatly parcelled and the roads logical and true. Only at the last minute does the parachutist realize that he is actually falling quite fast, as the ground appears to rush up to meet him. It is a powerful feeling that can induce fear and confusion and cause him to injure himself on landing.

It is sometimes like this with the best laid of plans. The commitment is real and apparently well thought through, but when it comes to action something strange seems to happen. This was the case with Lizzie, an executive taking on a demanding new role in a credit card company. 'All my good intentions disappear,' she complained, 'and my plans all go out the window!' Lizzie was an innovator, full of new ideas about how to change her team's working practices for the better, but she had to work with some very cautious, conservative colleagues who were used to working in a certain style. She devised a plan to cope with this situation, consisting of a weekly to-do list, indicating her priority tasks and the messages she wanted to communicate to her key interactors. It was all straightforward enough but in reality everything went awry. She would arrive at her coaching session, flushed, waving her hands and talking rapidly about the 'disasters' of the previous week before she had even sat down.

It was not as though Lizzie consciously doubted her action plan, but she seemed to jump from one activity to another, finishing nothing and then getting alarmed when work was requested that should have been completed. Rather than making her focus on a specific task, this kind of disturbance made her even more likely to change tack. At the same time, some of her strategies for communicating with the challenging individuals in the group were also going by the board. She seemed to be constantly choosing and re-choosing, rather than sticking to her well-founded plan of action.

There was nothing else to do in each session but take Lizzie through her to-do list and, calmly and patiently, point out how she needed to complete each ask. She would repeat the stages of the choice cycle like a mantra ('possibilize, probabilize, *actualize!*'). By the end of the session, she was calm, composed, motivated and, if anything, slightly ashamed of her 'fickleness', as she called it. Gradually, she started focusing on one task at a time, sticking to her weekly action plan religiously. She would regularly check if she was on course, revisiting the details of the plan if she was not. In this way, she was able to build up a reputation for delivering her tasks, which eventually meant that she could move on to the more creative aspects of her job.

Action as an escape from choice

If too little impetus to action can be a problem, then so can too much. Many an organizational project has had to be halted because belatedly someone asks the question: 'What exactly are we trying to achieve here anyway?' Only then does it dawn on the group that a project has been hurried into, without due reflection and attention to objectives, and because of this has to be started all over again. At an individual level, the impulse to rush into action can be similarly problematic.

Impulsiveness is an attempt to take a short cut through the choice cycle. The impulsive person's strong action-orientation and need to 'get on with things' can cause him to try to rush through the possibilizing and probabilizing stages of the choice cycle. Strategizing and objectives-setting are jettisoned, in favour of a headlong dash into action. This often results in a strange form of strategizing in reverse, in which one tries to figure out what one is aiming to do only as one is doing it, or even after it has been done! This excessive form of willpower can ride roughshod over the interests of others. Coaching impulsiveness of this kind often involves going back to the origins to find out what the client really wants and doesn't want and thus identify his future goals and expectations. In this way, a headlong drive for action can turn into something closer to authentic willpower, as the case below illustrates.

The case of Robin R.: From the funnel to the tunnel

Robin R. was a naval commando officer turned insurance salesman who was inclined to rush into actions without proper consideration. He took everything at a gallop; I could always recognize his quick steps on the floor as he approached the coaching room. According to his manager, Robin's impulsiveness had become a problem for his customers, who felt harassed by him, and for his colleagues, who were offended by him. Robin's reaction to others not being 'on the same wavelength' as him was blunt criticism and sometimes outright rudeness, which went against the people-centred culture of his firm.

When we looked at the way Robin made choices, it became clear that he seemed to hurtle straight from his first assessment of a situation into action itself. In terms of the Achievement Matrix, Robin went directly from Phase 1 (assessing what he wanted and didn't want) to Phase 8 (action itself). When we examined what was happening, Robin offered a number of excuses, all of which blamed others for his situation. But it was only when we focused on choice that Robin revealed his deep aversion to indecision. He related this to his military experience and cited several incidents where indecisive orders had caused injuries and perhaps cost lives. In his eyes, it was almost as though any decision was better than delay. It was hard to know what to make of Robin's attributions. It seemed to me that the challenges he was facing in his somewhat placid office in the Home Counties were substantially different from those presented by the tropical rainforests of Sierra Leone or the turbulent seas of the South Atlantic where he had developed his fervent dislike of indecision.

I decided to appeal to what Robin really wanted in his work. He said he wanted to be a success in his new career and learn new ways of getting on with people, which he finally admitted might have helped him progress further in the Navy. He was open about his problems with listening to others. He said his mind tended to race on from whatever the talker was talking about. So we began working on his listening skills, helping him to slow down and pay more attention to what was actually being said. Going through the choice cycle also helped him to identify how much he was missing out on in terms of accurate assessment and calculation.

The choice cycle can be envisaged as a funnel, narrowing from the widest range of possibilities at its mouth, through probable choices in the middle, to the selected action at its stem. I suggested to Robin that he was dispensing with possibilizing and 'going straight from the funnel to the tunnel', so to speak. This seemed to strike a chord with him. He admitted that exploring the possibilities of any given situation disturbed him but with a major effort he started trying to define decisiveness in favour of quality rather than velocity. He focused strongly on planning his interactions with customers, sometimes deliberately going back and forth through the choice cycle, making sure that he had captured every possibility. He did the same with colleagues and worked hard to remain calm, even though he didn't always feel that way. The change was not total. He was still recognizably himself in some ways: quick to make decisions and occasionally to criticize others. But he had moved himself into a more balanced style of interaction, where the drawbacks of his action orientation were outweighed by its advantages

In all the cases discussed above, clients have overcome the strong feelings of discomfort they experienced when trying to implement their choices. This is often an inevitable part of changing. In certain cases, however, this resistance may be telling the client that something is irrevocably wrong about her project. This possibility always hovers above the final stage of the choice cycle. But if a client's vision is not viable – and often it is only in action that we can really know this – it is important to acknowledge this in coaching and perhaps help her to find a new approach. After all, this kind of temporary setback is simply part and parcel of the continuous experiment that is human achievement.

Part 5

Coaching in the dimension of others

13

Coaching practical interactional expertise

In this chapter we return to the third aspect of the interactional self – its interpersonal dimension – and focus on coaching practical interactional expertise. Interacting effectively with others at work is about choosing what you want and integrating this with what others want. It involves achieving a personal dialectic between self and others, which is always a perilous balance: go too far towards the self and you fail to engage with others, like the leader who gets so far ahead of his followers that he loses sight of them; go too far towards trying to placate others and you can lose your independence and integrity.

Existential writers see this interaction in many different ways. For Heidegger (1962), being with others ('mitsein') is an indissoluble aspect of being human, while for Martin Buber (1958), the 'I' of the self can only be understood in relation to the 'thou' of the other. For Sartre, at least in his purely existentialist phase, the interaction of self and others is more heavily weighted on the side of the self. But the point these theorists make is the same: only in the process of relating to others do we truly become ourselves.

Every interactional coaching assignment is likely to develop the client's ability to relate to others, whether or not interpersonal expertise is identified from the outset as a primary coaching purpose. In this chapter, we look specifically at different practical techniques and approaches for coaching interactional competence, including planned interactions, perspective-switching, discovering hidden expertise and coaching through the coach–coachee relationship. We also explore skills coaching around interactional expertise, including camera-based work, and the kind of transformation that this can bring about for coachees.

Planned interactions

Discovering what the client really wants to achieve in relation to others is a crucial first step to coaching interactional expertise. This leads to mapping out his most influential relationships at work, as we examined earlier, which in turn is likely to prompt an exploration of the practical, interpersonal skills he will need to achieve his goals in relation to others. Many organizations recognize the significance of the self–others relationship through the many types of formal interactional training that they provide: interpersonal skills, influencing, relationship-building, personal impact, networking, presentation skills, and so on. In a group training context, however, it may not be possible to bind these general skills to the specific personality and objectives of an individual. Also, evaluating the significance of interpersonal competence sometimes suffers from an organizational tendency to rate 'soft skills' as less valuable than the 'hard skills' of technical expertise. In fact, as emotional intelligence research has suggested, interactional ability may be a far better predictor of overall organizational success than traditional IQ alone (Goleman et al., 2002). Coaching offers an opportunity to redress this balance by identifying and developing specific skills in a context where it is clear these skills are fundamental to the client's ability to achieve his ambitions at work.

Analysing interpersonal interactions in advance is another way to help the coachee to acquire practical interactional expertise. Paradoxically, the apparent spontaneity of many successful work interactions often turns out to be the product of careful planning. Executives who are expert at influencing and winning commitment from others often plan key interactions in advance, whether they are one-to-one conversations or large-scale meetings. Interpersonal effectiveness rarely happens by accident. One client, who complained that most of her meetings were 'a waste of time', began to change her attitude to them through coaching. 'I've always planned job interviews in minute detail or an important conversation with my boss,' she said, 'but up till now I haven't thought about most everyday meetings until they happen, even though that's where most of my job is done.'

Coaching through the coach–coachee relationship

Several ways of coaching interactional expertise exist within the coaching relationship itself. For example, the coach can use aspects of how she feels about the coachee and what she observes in the interaction between them to promote the coachee's skills. The coach may use this interaction as a model for other interactions or as a platform for exploring them. This may involve the communication aspects of the coaching dialogue, such as listening, questioning and speaking skills, which we'll cover in detail in the next chapter.

It also involves being aware of a client's body language. One client's very stiff, upright posture may seem inappropriate for conveying informality and warmth; another, who lies back in his chair with his legs extended in front him, may appear far too casual in his demeanour for the make-or-break negotiations he is about to engage in. Every facial gesture may be a clue as to where a client is in his personal dialectic of self and others. For example, whenever Brian spoke to me he looked past me or stared fixedly at a point on the floor. I found this lack of eye contact a little disconcerting but it seemed to fit the picture his HR director had given me of a highly intelligent executive who was failing to engage with his peers. When I pointed this out to Brian he didn't seem surprised – 'yes, my wife says that', he smiled – but I noticed after that he started to look at me much more frequently in our sessions.

What is going on outside is a sign of what is going on inside. Indeed, interacting with others can bring out some of our deepest emotions. Getting a client to describe his lived experience of an interaction in the coaching can be a way of identifying these feelings and the intentions behind them.

The coach may suggest that the client seems to be relying on the coach's judgment too extensively or imagining that the coach has all the answers. One client may reply 'yes, that makes me feel more secure' or another may say that the suggestion angers her because she dislikes being challenged. Such beginnings can lead to fruitful explorations.

Consider the case of Laura, to whom I said: 'I notice you seem to decide what you want to do in a coaching session and then change your mind. What's happening for you here?' She replied that initially she felt compelled to make quick decisions and that his gave her a great feeling of being in control, but as the session progressed she had an uncomfortable sensation that she was committing herself to something unachievable. This, she said, made her feel 'dizzy, not at all on top of things, like I'm floating'. Staying with this feeling in the coaching helped her identify it as something that consistently occurred with other people. She realized she was veering too violently between trying to assert her independence by making bold decisions and conforming to what she felt others wanted (in this case, her coach). Between pleasing herself and pleasing others, she was getting badly lost. Recognizing the complex emotional reality associated with this experiential state began to give her a new degree of control over it, which eventually manifested itself in more assured relationships with her colleagues.

Short, impromptu role-plays can also be useful. They direct emotional engagement towards a third party, which can be helpful for clients who find it hard to articulate their feelings to the coach. Simply asking a client to play out a few minutes of a conversation with a third party can be very revealing and may reveal the emotions and thoughts that are at stake in such interactions.

Perspective-switching ('empathy')

Another key interpersonal skill is the ability to switch perspectives with another person. This process of 'stepping into someone else's shoes' or 'seeing the world as another sees it', is a vital interpersonal asset but it is not something we literally can do, as ultimately we are confined to our own subjectivity. So how can we help a client to develop this intersubjective ability? One way is to visually demonstrate that the world looks different from different perspectives. The coach can do this by selecting an object in the coaching room, such as a lamp or a chair, and asking the client to describe it from different angles. This can bring home the extent to which we take for granted our ability to switch perspectives when experiencing the physical world.

What about helping the coachee to enter into the emotional world of other people? The ancient Greek root of the word 'empathy' means 'with feeling' and empathy involves attending to emotional signs in others as well as becoming aware of emotions in yourself that may be similar to those that others may be experiencing. For instance, you may have experienced disappointment at being turned down for a job you really wanted, which makes it easier to identify with someone in the same position. Or perhaps you have experienced disappointment in a totally different context but still can draw on that feeling. One client, who had tended to suppress his emotions in the belief that a totally rational style would work best with his peers, found that if he experimented with allowing these feelings to surface he actually had a much better sense of what motivated his colleagues: 'I try to locate an emotion in me that relates to what they might be experiencing.'

In fact, this approach resembles one of the techniques for developing 'emotional memory', by which the great acting coach, Stanislavski, helped actors to access specific feelings and moods. 'The problem,' he said, 'is to recapture an emotion that once flashed by like a meteor' (Stanislavski, 1937: 173). His solution was to think of a particular emotion as a bead that lies somewhere on a shelf or in a box in one of many rooms in one of many houses. By locating feelings in this way, an actor can build up a repertoire of emotions that can be used in different dramatic situations. For executives, too, this emotional versatility can be a real asset in creating insights into the behaviour of others.

Perspectivizing is not exclusively an emotional process, as ultimately it is about identifying the full range of the choices at play in an interpersonal situation. Clients who may have difficulty in expressing emotion in coaching may benefit from a more cognitive approach, which calls for strategic thinking. A client's interactional map is an ideal platform for this. Examining how different interactors may look at the same problem can reveal the different choices that confront them. This approach is similar to scenario-playing, strategic exercises in which executives may try to anticipate decision-making in an emergency or attempt to identify the dilemma that a commercial competitor is facing. It also strikes a chord with a technique found in marketing, as one client explained:

> If I'm considering a new product, I want to know
> everything about the potential customer. What they
> earn, what they eat and read, where they shop, etc., etc.
> It's not the details that matter; it's about getting into
> their minds, seeing their world as they see it.

The relevance of this approach to the world of coaching is obvious. It may be just the unexpected prompt that enables a coachee to unravel the hitherto baffling behaviour of a customer or colleague.

Hidden expertise

In my experience, clients often have the skills they need to achieve what they want at work without realizing it. This is often because their lives are compartmentalized between work and non-work activities. Helping to break down some of these inner walls in coaching can reveal interpersonal competences that already exist. Hidden expertise may be found in a hobby or leisure pursuit. For example, one coachee, a self-confessed 'indifferent manager', turned out to be an inspirational amateur football coach. The realization that he was getting more commitment from the under-privileged teenagers he coached on a football pitch than his own well-paid staff led him to drastically change his motivational methods at work. Another client found that reflecting on his experience as a parent opened new doors for him at work. He discovered a useful parallel between teaching his son to ride a bike and delegation: 'I had to protect him from hurting himself but in the end he had to learn to do it himself, even if that meant the odd bump and bruise.'

Another form of this 'domain-switching' is using previous work experience to create new insights into one's current situation. An interesting example of this is provided by Raul, who, as a young man, had served in the armed forces in Latin America:

> I was in the army twice, first in the infantry, then in intelligence. In intelligence everybody was equal, everybody was listened to. I often came up with suggestions that the whole unit accepted, even though I wasn't an officer. When I was in the infantry you did what you were told and that was it. Nobody cared a damn for your opinion and if you spoke up you got punished.

As Raul was now in a knowledge-based occupation that more closely resembled an intelligence unit than an infantry brigade, he started to use his experience of different types of organization to find more subtle and effective ways of managing his current relationships at work.

Interactional expertise and the sales model

Another powerful, unusual and thought-provoking way of coaching interpersonal expertise is through the model of sales. Selling is a highly interactional and choice-focused activity. The salesperson tries to help customers make the 'right' choices, in part by identifying what the customer wants (through expert listening and intelligent questioning). Common to interpersonal skills and selling are strategizing, targeting key individuals, intelligent questioning, persuasion and rapport-building. Even the lore surrounding the way a salesperson closes a deal can be seen as a series of techniques for easing or expediting another person's choice-making.

For some clients, using this model can remove some of the anxieties of relating to others. It seems to turn a 'soft' emotional issue into a 'hard', task-related matter and emphasizes how important it is to understand the motivations, desires and oppositions of others. This can be particularly helpful for people in non-sales roles such as administration, finance or IT. For them, 'selling themselves' may be regarded as 'selling out' and yet the ability 'to sell an idea' is crucial for everybody in the organization, from the CEO downwards. The ability to engage others is a vital occupational requirement, whether this is for the purpose of launching a new strategy, getting approval for budgets or simply conveying basic information.

Even sales-orientated executives often fail to realize that sometimes they have to sell themselves to colleagues as much as to customers. Like the contrast between the 'front of house' and 'back of house' behaviours studied by the interactional sociologist Goffman (1959), some executives appear to relax too much when they are not with customers. In so doing, they may neglect to apply their performance skills to colleagues, who may be just as influential as their external clients. The sales model also has an opposite extreme: executives who sell themselves too desperately, without consistency or principle. Such a coachee may be located too far towards the interpersonal pole of the self–others dialectic, in which case focusing on the self dimension, on his beliefs and values, can help to create a better personal balance. The eventual result may be a more authentic style of influencing other people's choices.

Perry's frown and the use of the camera in interpersonal skills coaching

Another technique for coaching interactional expertise is to use a camera and show clients the playback. US coaching authority Bruce Peltier (2001: 178) says of this approach: 'It has enormous potential for executive coaches and should be used with virtually every client.' This may be going a little far, in my view, as not all clients will choose to use this technique, but Peltier is definitely right about its potential and underutilization by coaches. Camera playback can be superb for showing the contrast between 'input and output' – what a situation feels like as opposed to what it looks and sounds like to others. Of course this can also be rendered by the coach's feedback, but playback gives the coachee the chance to hear and see herself and so make up her own mind. The biggest surprises – and sometimes the biggest changes – come from the coachee's realization of how she comes across to others. What may feel like a neutral expression to the client can look menacing or boring; what is experienced as a smile can look deadpan or mocking; what feels genuine may look insincere due to poor eye contact or incongruent hand gestures.

Perry's frown is a prime example. Perry was a policy advisor in the civil service who was confused by the reactions he often received from colleagues. When we recorded a short question and answer session with him a major reason for this confusion quickly became apparent. Perry had a habit of frowning at almost every question he was asked, which created an impression of disapproval. As he had a broad forehead and thick black eyebrows the effect was unmissable. In fact, Perry said his frowning had little to do with disapproval; it was more likely to be the result of uncertainty, weighing up a decision or concern at the questioner's possible reaction to his answer. With practice, he was able to correct this variance between the input and the output of his facial expressions and gain much more control of the impressions he was making on others.

Another advantage of practical skills is that it can bring out-of-session behaviour into the session. For example, a client might show nervousness in preparing for the role-play or try to put off the moment when he has to speak to the camera. One client subtly avoided watching himself on the playback, which led to a useful exploration of how he interpreted his body image and its place in his overall sense of himself.

It should be stressed at this point that inviting a client to engage in skills sessions, whether using the camera or not, should always be handled sensitively. It is an important part of the coaching choice process and one that can potentially help the client to build up his optative awareness. The advantage of placing choice at the forefront of human psychology in coaching is that it focuses coaches on the choices we are always making in life. The interactional approach shares with cognitive and behavioural models of coaching an appreciation of the importance of practical skills coaching, although with the emphasis on the coach as an equal partner in a process of choice. As we suggested earlier, person-centred coaches may object to skills coaching on the grounds that it is too 'directive' but I tend to go along with de Haan's (2008) view that coachees are psychologically robust enough to judge what they want and don't want to do. And in any case, we have no escape from choice, in coaching or anywhere else. In my view, being explicit about this process – making it indeed a central aspect of the coaching dialogue – is the best way to deal with decisions about what will work best for a client.

Towards the theatre of work: The case of Alan V. (continued from Chapter 1)

Several of these interpersonal coaching techniques, as well as aspects of the dialectic of self and others, come together in the case of Alan V., to which we can now return. He was an experienced IT manager from Newcastle, who worked for an American-owned media company, whose lack of 'personal profile' was causing him to lose out on promotion. Having failed to win promotion for the third year in succession, his manager was beginning to question whether Alan had a future in the company. The feedback Alan had received was that the senior managers on the promotion committee found him too 'unadventurous and dull' for a leadership role in an increasingly ambitious international company.

In my first session with Alan, I soon got a sense of what his manager was talking about. Alan's manner was very downbeat, his eye contact poor and his voice monotonous. He had interesting views about his company and a passion for music and sailing but he got bogged down too easily in specialist IT issues and often lapsed into silence. When I questioned myself as to what I was feeling in relation to Alan, the answer, regrettably, was 'boredom', an impression I only disclosed to him much later when I felt he would receive this feedback without offence.

'I'm 45, I'm not going to change the way I communicate with people now, am I?' This was Alan's first response when

I suggested we have a session on his communication skills, but he was intrigued by the prospect of working with a camera and agreed to it. When he presented a short formal business talk to camera, I was pleasantly surprised to discover that he used language in engaging and interesting ways and presented some stimulating arguments about IT. Yet when we tried an informal communication exercise, Alan reverted to his normal conversational mode: laconic, downbeat and detail-orientated. Comparing the two video clips was something of an eye-opener. Alan immediately recognized the attractiveness of his presentational style and the unappealing quality of his normal conversation: 'It *is* dull,' he says of the latter, 'I can see what they mean. I'm suffering from a charisma-bypass there!'

This insight was an important start for Alan. Why, I asked him, did he choose to communicate informally in this way? 'When you're presenting,' he replied, 'you've got to put on a show, that's accepted. But talking to people, well, that's who you are.' 'And who is that?', I asked, unable to resist the opportunity he had offered. He continued:

> I'm not a show boater. I don't like boasting or showing off. I'm not one of these people who are always promoting themselves, who love the sound of their own voice. I hate small talk. If I've got something to say, I say it, otherwise I shut up.

As we dug a little deeper, it seemed that Alan had pinpointed the opposite of what he wanted to be: the show-off, the small talker who dominates meetings and 'talks for the sake of talking'. Alan's normal mild manner gave way to a surpassingly fierce contempt for this oppositional self. Plainly, his view of how others should *not* behave had a powerful influence on how he thought *he* should behave. And there was another element in the conundrum that the playback brought out. Alan was convinced that senior managers should appreciate his value as a manager without his having to 'blow his own trumpet'. 'People should see what I do – my performance speaks for itself', he said. 'Managers are paid to see this kind of thing. I notice it in my own staff, why don't they?'

The more Alan articulated this view, the more resentful and resistant to change he became. I suggested that we look back at his interactional map and try to perspectivize from his senior managers' position. In doing so, it soon struck Alan that while it was relatively simple for him to pay close attention to his eight-person team, his senior managers had to engage with hundreds of different interactors in several countries. From this perspective, Alan saw that only those who stood out from the crowd were likely to be noticed. Using some ISO questions revealed Alan's very strongly introverted orientation. This revelation, perhaps paradoxically, helped him to feel more sympathy towards the extraverts in his company. He began to see them as different from him rather than 'wrong-headed', as he had previously thought.

I suggested that he observed some of the senior managers he admired in meetings. He began to appreciate the way intangible, seemingly pointless interventions can help to consolidate relationships. We worked on rapport-building conversations in role-plays and found ways in which Alan could develop small talk that he felt comfortable with, in order to open conversations with people he didn't know. In a breakthrough moment, he declared that he realized that work was a kind of theatre: 'Not just formal presenting, but every exchange you have, is a role you have to play, I suppose.' Much of the resentment he felt at being overlooked gave way to a whole-hearted commitment to networking with the influencers in the company. This he did with precision, carefully targeting key decision-makers and identifying the interactional style that would work best with them. Increasingly, this gave him the opportunity to engage effectively with his senior managers and express his opinions vigorously and with a measure of flair. In time, this new way of interacting with others brought him the promotion he wanted.

Alan's case underlines the value of practical interpersonal skills coaching. It challenges the mechanical, unreflective interpretation of 'skills acquisition' found in some models of learning prevalent in some organizations. In fact, skills coaching is a vibrant, unpredictable process with many possible outcomes. The client may discover skills he didn't know he possessed or conclude that he cannot learn the skills necessary to achieve his goals, prompting him to reassess them. Or he may find, in the safe 'virtual' reality of coaching, the opportunity to identify and overcome psychological issues before confronting the less forgiving world of the workplace. It is this plurality of choices that makes this type of learning so valuable.

14

Coaching communication skills

The subject of communication shines a particularly strong light on our human role as choice-makers in interaction. Communication fully involves the interactional self, as it is about interacting with others and interacting with yourself, in time and through your bodily presence. These interactions all involve choices, such as 'who should I interact with?', 'how do I want to come across to my audience?' and 'what are my main messages?' Effective communicators are skilled at making these kinds of choices. Ineffective communicators make either the wrong choices – for instance, preferring what interests *them* rather than what interests their interactors – or no choices at all, hoping their interactors will decide what is important, which may be asking a little too much.

Interactional coaching prioritizes communication expertise, in part because it is so central to an executive's success and in part because it can be such a rich source of personal and interpersonal change. Some coaches using other models may feel that they lack the competence to coach communication skills. In fact, at the heart of communication expertise is an aptitude for listening, questioning and stating, which is probably common to every coaching practice. At any rate, these are the main skills that we'll concentrate on in this chapter, as well as looking at the advantages of practical communication work in highlighting the client's usage of language and its beneficial effects in 'forcing' choices that might not otherwise be made.

Coaching listening skills

The importance of good listening skills for executives is hard to overstate. As we have already observed in several cases, learning to listen to others – and to yourself – is a vital part of being able to achieve what you want at work. It is also a key leadership competence. Yet, in my experience, many executives overrate their listening skills.

The coach generally gains a good sense of how the coachee listens to others by the way she listens to him. Highlighting this may be enough to help the client improve her listening. Alternatively, listening skills can be coached more formally, probably as a short stint within a longer coaching session. Keeping skills development within the coaching process can be an advantage to executives, who may want to keep this shortcoming to themselves. Listening exercises and role-plays focus on helping clients to become aware of the process of open listening and the choices they are making in the course of it. A key listening aptitude, the reader may recall, is choice-deferral, which is setting aside initial choices as possibilities rather than unconsciously endorsing them as actualities and thereby jumping to conclusions. The evidential and conclusive stages of listening also need to be emphasized, because they establish an enquiring mode that helps the listener move towards the best possible interpretation of what she is hearing.

Max was an example of a promising young executive whose career progress was seriously threatened by his inability to listen to others. He had a rare talent for 'unlistening': failing to concentrate on what his interactor was saying, interrupting their sentences and constantly consulting his Blackberry. His main unlistening technique was his quick-fire interpretation of the motives of others. 'I know why you've referred to that', he would say to me, and then give me a reason utterly unconnected with my real intention. Speaking about a colleague, he said confidently: 'I didn't give him a real hearing because I immediately guessed his real reasons for blocking my budget.' It soon became obvious that what Max called his 'mindreading ability' was based less on evidence than on his fertile imagination. We started going through the basic processes of listening, which encouraged him to hold back on his instantaneous choices about his interactor's meaning and to question himself and others before reaching a conclusion. In this way, slowly but surely, he began to connect with what others around him were really saying.

Coaching questioning skills

Questioning is another extremely important executive competence. Good questions can be used to expand, contract or implement choices at work. They can open up subjects that were previously concealed, reveal new pathways, reinforce methodologies and instil an enquiring organizational climate. At each stage of the choice cycle certain types of enquiry are appropriate. Questions at the possibilizing stage tend to explore new territories, stimulate imagination or encourage innovation. At the probabilizing stage the enquiry is more directive, with questions that move towards decisions, while questions around implementation are likely to be even more closed.

The interactional coach models this kind of questioning as part of the basic coaching dialogue and often this is sufficient for the client to modify her questioning style. For instance, one client particularly liked the 'into the future questions' that his coach had asked him, which try to identify a person's goals and stance towards the future. Another client said he was experimenting with the feelings-related questions he had observed in his coaching.

Sometimes, coaching questioning expertise needs to take a more direct approach. This was true in the case of Terri, a sales director whose management style seemed to be stifling her team's sense of initiative. In our first session, she unleashed a salvo of closed questions including: 'What percentages of the people you've coached have been in my industry sector?' 'How many psychology degrees do you have?' 'Should I expect to see changes immediately?' I almost felt I was under police interrogation and I suspected she probably made her direct reports feel much the same.

This impression was substantiated by the three questions that Terri said she regularly asked her team: 'How much did that deal earn us?' 'Did that push your team up the ranking table?' 'Why didn't that work?' The trouble with these questions was that they focused entirely on the results of the team's initiatives and not on the choice-making process that produced them. When we brainstormed opposite ways of talking to the team, Terri quickly came up with the following alternatives:

- What was your thinking behind that initiative?
- What were the main dilemmas you faced in coming to that conclusion?
- What was the main thing you learned from that project?

Armed with these new questions and, just as important, a genuine desire to listen to the answers, Terri began to positively transform her relationship with her team.

Coaching speaking skills

Effective speaking is about authentically interacting with others. Communicating your message effectively involves knowing what you want to say in different interpersonal situations and being able to say it in a way that engages, informs and persuades your audience. In many ways, goal-driven communication is about trying to make others choose the choices you have chosen, and the stakes can be high. Willpower may not be enough to ensure that your messages are not misinterpreted and the most whole-hearted commitment to an argument will not necessarily ward off the possibility of painful rejection.

From the interactional perspective, coaching speaking skills involves three areas of significance: strategy, content and delivery. The strategic element of effective communication starts with the question: Who are you trying persuade? This may seem obvious but many people tend to focus first on what they want to say, without realizing that their message is always directed at a specific audience and will vary from audience to audience. For example, a set of messages that may work for your boss may be quite wrong for your customers. It is also important to analyse the situation of the communication, finding out, for example, the degree of formality or informality it involves. In this manner, you can feel your way into your interactional situation and begin to accurately shape your communication before you have even consciously started to develop the content.

This was missing from Simon's approach to presentations. He was a brilliant financial analyst but his talks were poorly received. His audience seemed to be confused, bored or annoyed by them. When we explored his communication strategy, it became clear that he organized his presentations according to his own academic preferences. Yet, he admitted, his audiences were fairly unacademic: some were novices in his subject, some generalists; very few were experts. In fact, most were commercially orientated. In a sense, Simon was making choices around an imaginary academic audience rather than the real audiences in front of him. Helping him to see things from his actual audience's perspective enabled him to start changing his talks so that they became more relevant and engaging.

'What are you trying to persuade your audience to do?' is a question that relates to the content of a talk or set of messages. This is where choice-making is most acute. It involves selecting your single most important message and backing it up with a clear argument. Identifying your lead message is very helpful, because prioritizing is the basis of effective communication. So knowing who you are, what you want and who you need to influence all come together very intensely around the headline message you would want everybody to remember. Important as this logical and focused framework is, you also need to use the expressive potential of language to the full, through examples, metaphors and stories. This can help to earn your interactor's attention and make your argument more memorable.

Communication expertise can be coached by simply working through what a client intends to say in a meeting or formal presentation. For instance, it was soon apparent that Gillian had a great deal to say about her new change programme for her operations team but no real sense of what her priorities were. She seemed to roam from subject to subject without a clear course. When I pointed this out, she said: 'I'm leaving it up to the group to take what they want from it, I suppose.' While this democratic style of choice-making may have been appropriate in another context, it seemed at odds with the important announcement she wanted to make. In fact, it seemed more like an evasion of choice. When I asked her to tell me the one sentence from her entire talk that she wanted the group to remember, she quickly decided on: 'This change cannot happen without your participation.' With her lead message established, her other main points quickly fell in behind it, producing a far more impressive and persuasive argument than before.

'How do you want to get your message across?' is a question that raises the issue of delivery. This final aspect of spoken communications is far more important than is commonly assumed. According to some research, anything up to 66% of the overall impression that you make on others is non-verbal (Birdwhistell, 1970). The significance of non-verbal communication, especially body language and vocal expression, is now a well-established area of practical study by psychologists and others. It provides an empirical counterpart to the philosophical point that Merleau-Ponty (1962: 88) makes when he says that human reality is 'not a psyche joined to an organism but the movement to and fro of an existence which at one time allows itself to take corporeal form and at others moves towards personal acts'. As 'body-subjects', our perception of logical, rational messages is only a fraction of our experience of others. We make our choices around many other things, especially our feelings about the person delivering the message. So eye contact, smiling, gesturing and using your voice to convey differing emotions all have a huge effect in persuading us to accept or reject someone's point of view.

Many of us have experienced subject matter that may be interesting when read but comes across as dry or irrelevant in a spoken context. Executives often commit this 'content fallacy': the belief that your content somehow will speak for itself. This is in part an extreme prioritization of writing over speaking. At worst, it is a form of solipsism, as though others will understand what I have to say simply because I think it! In fact, a 'good' message delivered in a 'bad' way – in a manner interpreted as angry, morose, cynical or arrogant –

can be transformed into a bad message. That is how far the communication compass can spin.

Coaching with a camera can be particularly useful in this context. For example, Nancy was delivering a speech that was intended to motivate her software engineering team after a very difficult period for them. She had worked hard on the content and analysed her audience, picking out the team members she specifically wanted to influence, but her speech came across as lifeless and distant. Why? When we looked at the camera playback, we both agreed that it was because she wasn't smiling enough or looking at her audience, and there was a lack of vigour in her voice. 'It looks like I don't really believe what I'm saying', she observed. When she rehearsed the speech again, she was much more positive and energetic in her vocal tone, with more smiling, emphatic hand gestures and reassuring glances at the audience. As a result, the talk seemed to be totally transformed, even though its content was virtually identical to Nancy's first attempt.

The language of self and others

Another advantage of working on communication skills is that it enables the coach to explore the client's use of language, which will always be fundamental to our way of relating to ourselves and to others. For instance, the kind of stories a client tells in preparing a talk may say a good deal about how she thinks about herself. Are they stories that show her in a good light or a bad light? Do her narratives build her up or put her down? Vocabulary, and even sentence structure, can also be significant. When articulating his vision, one client used such convoluted, management-speak phraseology, with so many impersonal constructions, that it seemed he had no personal ownership of it. Every time he used a word like 'disintermediate', when he actually meant 'bring people together', I suspected that his real message was going to be lost on his team.

Metaphors can be particularly rich in meaning. They can reveal how clients see themselves and how they expect others to see them. One client, who was involved in corporate strategy, was fond of martial metaphors to describe his world-view. His language was replete with terms like 'ambush', 'counter attack', 'all-out war', 'generals and foot soldiers'. A client in sales described his role in terms of hunting, using phrases such as 'stealth tactics', 'pursuing a sale', 'blood in the water', 'you only get one shot, so make it count'. By contrast, a client in human resources tended to use words derived from horticulture, such as nurturing, growing and sowing seeds. 'These are tender shoots,' he said about the participants of his graduate programme, 'put them out in the cold too early and they'll wither.' Such metaphors take us to the heart of a client's sense of self but also indicate ways in which they can best interact with others. Plainly, using martial or hunting imagery may create quite the wrong impression for people who see their work as a developmental, nurturing process.

'Forcing' choices

Focusing on communication in coaching can be extremely useful in helping a client to find his personal dialectic, the point of balance where he most feels himself. For instance, it can be a very useful way of achieving the right level of inter-action between positivity and negativity in the impressions one creates on others. Too much negativity and the speaker is likely to undermine her own argument, but an over-positive style can come across as slick or insincere.

Coaching communication can also help in 'forcing' choices that the client might not otherwise be able to make. This happens particularly when focusing on the advantages of conciseness in speaking. In oral communication what you leave out is as important as what you leave in, a point that further underscores the crucial role of renunciation in choice-making. Encouraging a client to express herself in a short talk – perhaps as short as two minutes – can help her to choose what is really essential about a subject. Presentations and communication in general often fail because there is too much indecision built into the speaker's words. This can be compared to a proliferation of road signs that are intended to make it easier to reach a destination but actually make it harder. Focusing on what the coachee really wants to say and the impression she wants to create in her audience can promote clinical choice-making that cuts through to what really matters.

In fact, coaching communication skills can accelerate the choosing process in unexpected ways. As communication is an emotional, cognitive, behavioural and physical process, the choices it brings to the surface can involve any aspect of the client's being. John's planned presentation to his executive committee reveals this very clearly. In his coaching, he had been extremely optimistic about his presentation, with its bold messages and ambitious scope. However, when John rehearsed his talk to camera, he became uncharacteristically hesitant, almost faltering in his manner. This was immediately obvious to him on the playback and in trying to explain it he began to realize just how flawed his proposal was. Happily, at this stage, nothing had been lost and he was able to work out a much subtler, more compelling plan that had a far better chance of success. He said he had been aware of the logical shortcomings of his plan but only at a pre-reflective level, which he called 'a vague feeling in my bones'. You might say that rehearsing his presentation enabled him to realize what his body 'knew' and his mind did not, which is further testimony to the usefulness of coaching in this way.

15

Coaching around conflict

So far we have looked at coaching aspects of interactional expertise, where executives choose to improve their ways of relating to others. But what happens when others are hostile to a coachee's choices and significant areas of his interactional map seem to be dominated by individuals who are set against each other? Choices that are not reciprocated, or even seen as choices, can lead to a denial of freedom, which is one of the most damaging of human experiences. When conflict is the primary trigger for a coaching assignment, other issues tend to fall into the background.

Many forms of conflict rear their head in organizations and consequently find their way into the coaching room. In this chapter, I want to highlight three types: unavoidable conflict; conflict based on failed recognition; and conflict as a power struggle, which is perhaps the most intense and potentially destructive of interactions.

Unavoidable conflict

Existential thinking sees human reality as a dialogue with others. 'Authentic interaction,' writes Bo Jacobsen (2007: 60), 'lets the human being emerge in its entirety, freely and responsibly.' This kind of interaction flows from the understanding that others are an indissoluble part of our own existence. We cannot escape our interconnection with others; even solitude is defined by the very absence of others. But it follows from this that there is always a potential for conflict in human interaction. My choices and your choices may well compete with each other. I might try to influence you to do what I would like you to do but if I fail to recognize that you have a free choice about this then the trouble starts. Once we deny another's freedom, the boundary of mutual recognition has been overstepped and conflict is often the result.

If the inevitably conflictive aspects of social interaction are experienced as avoidable, the consequences can be painful. Consider the case of Andy, an operations executive who dreaded conflict with his colleagues. He seemed to take personal responsibility for almost any disagreement at work and in consequence he experienced intense feelings of guilt and inadequacy. When we analysed several of these 'confrontations', as he called them, they seemed to arise more or less inevitably from the tasks of his supervisory role, such as asking for documents, imposing deadlines or reporting inappropriate behaviour. Andy was distressed by these interactions and yet, as he admitted after a few sessions, some of what he experienced as aggression by others could easily be described as 'everyday give and take' or 'harmless banter'. Only when he started to separate the types of robust interaction that were part of his job from real acts of hostility could he regain some enjoyment from his work.

Conflict as failed recognition

As Andy's story suggests, conflict at work can sometimes be a matter of misinterpretation, at least in part. Indeed, as an experienced HR director once said to me: 'You should never underestimate people's capacity to misunderstand one another.' Such cases may be clarified relatively easily in coaching but the failure to see the other as a person in their own right can be more difficult to resolve. Existentially, the ideal position is outlined by Laing (1960: 22) when he says: 'The other is seen by me as a person as responsible, capable of choice, in short, as a self-acting agent.' Failure to recognize the other's choices and responsibilities can seem like a denial of their freedom. Of course, there are always likely to be some people with whom we may find it difficult to work, but that does not necessarily entail conflict. However, when someone is taken for granted, or false assumptions are made about them, a much greater sense of threat may be experienced. This can quickly harden into a much more impenetrable opposition, as negative action produces a negative reaction and misunderstanding spirals into outright hostility.

Recognizing other people's freedom of choice is the basis of much of the law in Western democracies, so it seems right that this should be the basis of successful interaction at work. Yet this is not always respected by those who are in positions of authority in organizations and this can provoke anger, resentment and frustration among employees. Perhaps an evolutionary psychologist would argue that these kinds of emotion alert us when our choice-making capacity is being severely limited by our environment, and as such are useful to survival. However, this does not make these feelings any easier to tolerate. Organizationally, this kind of denial can lead to demoralization, resistance and even deliberate sabotage, which acts as a reminder that we all have choices about how to act, even in the most oppressive circumstances.

Something of the phenomenology of anger at work is illustrated by Joel, a talented financial administrator who was plagued by bouts of frustration that he found increasingly difficult to contain in the workplace. The causes of his anger seemed to be related to his feeling that his individuality was being denied by others. He became angry when criticized, as he was frequently, particularly by his manager. In the longer term, these 'attacks', as he called them, made him mildly depressed. 'They make me feel I've got nowhere to go and nothing I can do,' he said, 'I'm just trapped and the only way out is by getting angry.'

Joel also experienced anger when he wasn't listened to. Several of his colleagues would superficially give him a hearing but they didn't appear to acknowledge what he was saying:

> They just dismiss me, as though it was me who's the problem. I end up rambling and even ranting. And that I suppose confirms what they thought in the first place, that I wasn't worth listening to.

He said he felt completely isolated, so much so that he stopped even trying to confide in others. The significance of listening as a basic human right in the workplace is clearly illustrated by this. 'They don't have any idea what's going for me in this job,' he complained, 'and the kind of decisions I have to make on my own.' It is no coincidence that Joel said that the most valuable aspect of his coaching was 'being listened to'. This was closely related to his profound sense of being taken for granted at work. 'If I stay late it's because there's work to be done,' he said, 'not because I've got nothing else to do in my life. But they seem to take it as read that I'll be here.' I got the sense that Joel's colleagues thought of him as a kind of work-machine, without any options or possibilities of his own.

Coaching for Joel was focused on acknowledging his right to make choices and his need to manage his emotions, as he clearly did not help himself by getting angry with his colleagues or sulkily withdrawing from them. He gained the confidence to openly state his grievances to his manager in a controlled way, which seemed to have a positive effect on her. Through a range of tactics Joel also made it clear that he was not always available to work late without prior consultation. Indeed, by starting to leave work on time, the whole department was forced to change its routine. For a while things improved, but Joel's resentment of the way in which he'd been treated was never far from the surface. Eventually, he came to the conclusion that the right choice for him was to resign from his job. He did this with a calm dignity that suggested he had learned lessons from this experience that he would be able to put to good use in the future.

Conflict as a struggle for power

At its most extreme, workplace competition can spiral into conflict and a destructive struggle for domination. In these circumstances, an executive's desires are often blocked by the deliberate opposition of another person or group. Clients who seek only to dominate others can turn organizations into battle fields from which few can escape. Ritualistic fights for territory are part of the fabric of everyday life in some companies. In coaching, a highly conflictive executive often resonates through a coachee's interactional map, creating a ripple effect that is felt a long way from its point of origin. It sometimes seems that it is this executive, perhaps the client's boss or his boss's boss, who is the real subject of the coaching because of the frequency with which the conversations return to him.

In the existential tradition, no-one analyses the struggle for power more vividly than Sartre. In *Being and Nothingness* (1958) he outlines a kind of master and slave conflict, where each person is the loser in an ontological zero-sum game. According to this, what we want from others is for them to recognize our freedom: our right to see the world differently, to have different desires and to make choices based on them. If we are denied this recognition as individuals we will struggle to achieve it, in whatever way we can. This can turn into a vicious circle. If the look of the other deprives me of my freedom, I can only retrieve this by stealing the freedom of the other. In this world, sadism and masochism become a model for love, and at times the political power games of organizations seem to echo this reality rather more than some would like to admit.

And yet a few years later, in a work only published after his death, Sartre (1992) himself provides a solution to this apparently intractable power struggle: 'the appeal'. Based on Hegel's concept of mutual recognition, this process has been summarized as follows: 'one appeals to another person by inviting her to cooperate towards a joint end' (Heter, 2006: 35). The appeal is based on the recognition of human diversity, since it recognizes that we must start from the differences that exist between people and find what we have in common with them rather than assuming that this commonality already exists. What we always have in common with others is an end, a goal, which in itself has human value. The appeal, Sartre suggests, also acknowledges the significance of ambiguity, as 'the recognition of ambiguity, since it recognizes the other's freedom in a situation . . . is itself a form of reciprocity from the moment it springs up' (Sartre, 1992: 499).

This process of appealing to a shared project and common goals is a key to coaching conflict resolution.

Recognizing the other's goals is itself positive and focusing on common ground breaks down the isolation of individuals, who may be in danger of succumbing to an individualistic, Hobbsian 'war of all against all'. By recognizing that we may have something in common, we go some way towards recognizing the legitimacy of the differences that separate us. But the appeal is not without risk. By appealing to the other, I risk rejection and potentially a worsening of the conflict. And yet it is precisely this risk that gives value to the appeal, making it a reciprocal interaction rather than a mere demand.

Case study: Ross and the battle of the borders

My first impression of the interaction between Ross and Guy, partners in a large Midlands law firm, was that they were engaged in a vicious power struggle. I was called in to coach Ross, a long-established partner who wanted to update the firm's marketing and development practices in a way that maintained its traditions. But I had also been briefed on his conflict with Guy, a new partner who had recently joined from another, more commercially assertive firm. In our first session, Ross said that Guy aimed to replace him as the leading force in the modernization project and even drive him out of the firm altogether. The partners had reached the point where they were openly scornful of each other, which was causing confusion and distress in their teams, who were breaking into increasingly hostile opposing camps.

Ross seethed with rage when talking about Guy. He saw him as an unethical, 'profiteering' type of lawyer and, it has to be said, 'very English', whereas Ross saw himself as 'typically Scottish'. Anything Ross proposed was immediately vetoed by Guy. This was 'politically motivated,' Ross claimed, 'a blatant attempt to uproot me from all places of influence in the firm.' In coaching, as we know, open listening is very important but so is evidential listening and, after a while, I was keen to find concrete evidence for Ross's opinions. In reply, Ross recounted a number of relatively small incidents that seemed to loom large in his mind and concluded by exclaiming: 'I just knew the moment I first saw

Guy that he was out to get one over on me.' As a lawyer, Ross had a reputation for meticulously assembling case evidence, but in some of his relationships with colleagues he seemed to rely heavily on gossip and the interpretation of ambiguous signs. When I suggested this to him, he was visibly shocked but it appeared to start him thinking about the choices he was making.

The next challenge was the appeal, finding a purpose or goal that Ross shared with Guy. The modernization of the firm was the obvious candidate but initially Ross said this was merely a cover for Guy's personal ambitions. At the same time, Ross was acutely aware that the conflict between the partners was damaging morale in their respective teams and that their reputations were suffering. So he agreed to give the appeal a chance and invited Guy for lunch. Still sceptical of Guy's professional motives, he first tried to establish common ground in their private lives and soon found that they shared a passion for golf. The next stage was to talk through their respective modernization plans. For this, Ross somewhat reluctantly accepted a colleague's offer to facilitate a meeting between him and Guy. To his surprise, Ross discovered that he and Guy held similar views on the overall destination of the firm, even though they held diametrically opposite opinions about how to get there. They decided not to try to resolve this latter issue for the time being. In short, they 'agreed to disagree' – an interesting everyday phrase that implies a mutual recognition of difference and of the rights of the other to hold opposing views. Ross also tried to find ways to bring the partners' respective teams together in order to defuse the animosity that had developed between them.

Ross now started to experiment with his new hypothesis that Guy was more motivated by the best interests of the firm than his own ambitions. If this was true, Guy's 'plotting' could be construed as a defensive reaction to Ross's apparent hostility. Changing his choices in this way was not easy for Ross. Several times he relapsed into distrust of his colleague, but fortunately Guy appeared to be responsive to Ross's attempts to change and made significant concessions to him over the firm's modernization. The negative cycle of interpretation started to unwind. The partners found a series of compromise measures and, in time, built up an effective professional relationship that was recognized throughout the firm. Ross never entirely freed himself of his suspicions of Guy but if he had doubts he would discuss them openly with him. A workable, mutual trust had been achieved.

The importance of trust

Working with intense conflict can be difficult. The dialectic of trust and mistrust in working situations can be explosive. Many years ago, Shakespeare brilliantly illustrated this in depicting the betrayal of Othello by his erstwhile lieutenant, Iago, who himself felt betrayed by his general's failure to promote him. Trust lost in this way can be lost forever. In coaching, a client's belief that human interactions are all about winning and losing can threaten to turn the coaching relationship itself into a cauldron of trust and mistrust. One way in which the coach counters this is by aligning his choices with the client's, as far as this is possible. Ideally, both coach and coachee have the same purpose, to achieve what the coachee wants to achieve. This particular model of interaction at work is fairly unique in organizations, as in reality there will always be an element of competition between employees' goals. But the mutual recognition of the coaching process can offer the coachee a rare opportunity to rediscover his ability to trust other people – or even to find it for the very first time.

Part 6

Coaching leadership and managerial expertise

16

Coaching leadership

Leadership development is implicit in all interactional coaching and promoting personal and collective leadership is one of its three main goals. It is easy to overexaggerate the differences between leaders and other executives, because in a sense we are all leaders in our own lives. And yet there is something about the quantity and quality of the choice that organizational leaders make that is genuinely different. Not only are there more of these choices, but they are often more complicated and, most crucially, have more impact on more people. If you or I get a decision wrong, we may affect no-one but ourselves. Yet the leader of a large organization or corporate division may have tens of thousands of employees to settle with if her choices turn out to be wrong, not to speak of shareholders, suppliers and other stakeholders. The pressure of leadership, at its most extreme, was well described by Sartre when he wrote about the 'anguish' of a military leader, making decisions on which the lives of his soldiers depend:

> All leaders know that anguish. It does not prevent their
> acting, on the contrary it is the very condition of their
> action, for the action presupposes that it is a plurality
> of possibilities, and in choosing one of these they
> realize that it has value only because it has been
> chosen. (1948: 32)

In short, the leader's choices have no guarantees. Of course, on the whole, corporate life does not involve life or death decisions but all leadership potentially stretches choice-making to the limits. As one client put it, it's 'the big choosing'. This is one reason why interactional coaching is well suited to working with leadership situations. Theoretically, its focus on choice-makers in interaction puts leadership into perspective; practically, its wide range of techniques, from strategic development to practical skills coaching, helps to engage leaders, who may feel their status implies they have no need of coaching.

In this chapter, we look at how the choice cycle can be used to identify different types of leadership style and explore the case of an executive whose desire to lead was so intense that it threatened to defeat him. We start by examining some of the challenges of coaching leaders via the three lenses of the interactional self.

Leadership and the interactional self

Time

Time is at the forefront of leadership. One of the leader's most established attributes is to guide others into the uncertainty of the future. In a real sense, he exists in order to choose the future, either by persuading others to follow his vision or by helping others to arrive at their own. At the same time, leaders must achieve an acceptable interpretation of the past. In some cases this might be a clean break, using the past as a template of what not to do, or it may be the opposite, an attempt to return to core values that have been abandoned. Or perhaps it is a matter of synthesizing the past, taking the best of what has occurred and jettisoning the rest. Either way, through their future choices, leaders aim to bring out the full potential of the present.

What the leader wants is crucially important. The first cardinal question is as relevant here as in any other role and yet the answer can easily be taken for granted. Identifying the degree of convergence between what a leader wants and the everyday choices she is making is also vital, as is understanding the character of her desire for leadership. Some executives exhibit a strong impulse to lead from the onset of their careers or even from childhood; others are more contingent in their desires, only developing an ambition to lead when a concrete opportunity appears before them.

Time also plays its part in the mechanics of coaching leaders, as their often frantic schedules may require flexibility on the part of the coach. The ability to engage a client rapidly may also come into play, especially where she has doubts about the opportunity cost of coaching. The coach also needs to be open to the dramatic changes that often occur in a leader's world, while maintaining a consistency of purpose. Helping the client to find 'the still point in the turning world', in the words of T.S. Eliot (1941), is a greater challenge than ever in this coaching purpose.

Self

Under the pressure of leadership, an executive's values and beliefs can be threatened, compromised or even brought to the point of collapse. Self-analysis can help to evaluate the way the leader's choice landscape may change dramatically as a result of choices forced on him by the reality of taking charge. For example, longer working hours may pressurize the interaction between a leader's professional and private life, which can lead to intense emotional pressures and dilemmas. Choices may hang over him even in his leisure time and this can be stressful. At the other end of the spectrum, leadership can induce a kind of euphoria and a new sense of potency, especially when things are going well. This can also change a leader's values, for better or for worse.

Inevitably, personality factors play a part in leadership. For example, extraverts may find it difficult to take in their stride the sense of isolation that senior jobs often induce, as they discover they are unable to fully confide in others or explain what is at stake in major decisions. For introverts, on the other hand, the amount of socializing that leadership involves may be the main challenge: learning to live under the constant gaze of others. For this kind of executive, coaching is often about helping them to deal with increased social activity in a way that works for them. For instance, one very reserved chief executive who tried to engage his staff spontaneously through 'managing by walking around', eventually found that he interacted with them more successfully through regular, structured meetings than by attempting to be someone he was not.

Others

Perhaps the biggest impact of leadership comes with the expansion in the leader's interaction with others. The typical chief executive's interactional map reveals the width and depth of the web of influence with which she has to work. This may include her chairman, shareholders, executive and non-executive board members, customers, suppliers, the media, equity analysts, the general public, as well as her team and other staff members. Business coaches Shaw and Linnecar (2007) suggest that a typical CEO has 14 different types of stakeholder, and even this may be a conservative estimate. The choices a leader makes in this densely layered, ambiguous interpersonal situation will ultimately define his or her leadership and may call for a new form of multi-perspective expertise. This requires a skill set that is akin to plate-spinning, in that it involves keeping many plates spinning at the same time but with a clear sense of which plates can and cannot be allowed to fall. What the senior manager's interactional map often reveals is that it is a mistake to think that leadership is first and foremost about managing downwards, as many leadership theorists imply. Of course, a CEO's staff hugely influence her chances of success but they do not directly hire her or fire her, or decide on her level of reward. Senior managers' own choices often reflect this. For example, recent research indicates that 38% of CEOs prioritize their shareholders above their employees, as opposed to only 13% who said their staff came first (Tappin and Cave, 2008). In practical terms, these real choices often have to be the starting place for leadership coaching, rather than the choices the coach might prefer a leader to be making. At the same time, the coach should never continue with a coaching project if he feels genuinely uncomfortable with it from an ethical viewpoint.

If creating the right balance between his interactors is one great challenge for a leader, finding the right dialectic between self and others is another. Following his own desires is a powerful motivator that a leader may well need, not least to prevent him from surrendering his will to shareholders or other powerful influences within the organization. And yet prioritizing one's own desires at the expense of others can also lead to irresponsible leadership. This psychological dimension is important – Lee (2003) captures the same dialectic in more psychodynamic terms when he speaks of the opposition of 'defiant' and 'compliant' leadership – and can sometimes be missed in purely business-orientated approaches to leadership coaching.

The choice cycle and the biases of leadership

What does the choice cycle tell us about coaching leaders? For a start, it enables us to form an ideal, synthetic model of leadership. According to this, the complete leader is able to combine the skills associated with the three stages of the cycle: possibilizing, probabilizing and actualizing. The first skill set involves strategizing, imagining and inspiring; the second is directed towards working with existing resources realistically and mobilizing the team; and the third implies the ability to effectively put strategies into practice. This model can be useful in coaching because it helps to identify the extent to which a coachee is biased towards one or other of these leadership styles and the strengths and weaknesses that this implies. The possibilizing leader may be very strategic but not sufficiently practical or interpersonally skilled to implement strategy; the probabilizer may be expert at organizing resources, both human and material, but unadventurous in strategy and lacklustre at implementation. Finally, the actualizing leader may excel in action but is potentially weak in strategy or consensus-building.

The leader as possibilizer

Let's begin with the possibilizing leader. Possibilizers are most comfortable at the identification stage of the choice cycle, questioning and challenging the status quo. They work well with big picture thinking and they champion change. They can get people thinking differently, tapping into new possibilities and expanding their horizons. At their best, possibilizers inspire others with a new confidence in their own ability. Barack Obama's 2008 presidential campaign slogan, 'yes we can', is a classic possibilizing statement.

The challenges for this type of leader come with the next two stages of the choice cycle. Possibilizers may find it difficult to make collective decisions. They may prefer abstract choices to concrete ones and, when it comes to implementing their choices in real situations, they may not be equal to the politics of change, the frustration of small details and the quirkiness of events.

This was Roberto's predicament. He ran a digital TV company whose viewing figures were going down fast. He had a reputation in advertising as a brilliant brand strategist and in television as an outstanding scheduler of programmes, but his inability to commission successful new programmes was letting him down badly. He had lost the confidence of his staff and his office was being referred to as 'the ivory tower'. The problem was that the innovative programming decisions made by Roberto and his creative team were entirely left to his inexperienced producers to implement. This allowed Roberto to absorb himself in his next, hugely ambitious strategic project or intellectually impressive conference speech. Had his new programmes been successful, no doubt his delegation style would have been lauded, but the viewing figures for them were little short of calamitous. Through coaching, Roberto recognized that he needed to turn his attention to the actual process of developing programmes. He needed to bring some order to his warring management team and engage more with his producers and with real TV viewers. This was a major struggle but he gradually started to become more adept at all-round choice-making. As a result, the staff's expertise and motivation increased, as in time did the company's programme ratings.

The leader as probabilizer

Probabilizers are masters of the contingent. They excel in the nitty gritty of diplomacy, practical decision-making and planning. At any time there may be many things that might be done, but what can actually be achieved? That is when the probabilizer comes to the fore, making happen what can happen.

Probabilizers recognize the power of necessity and the urgency of the immediate. If, as Kierkegaard (1980: 49) suggests, anxiety is 'the intermediate term' between possibility and actuality, you can say that probabilizers are experts in getting the best out of anxiety. They use it to bring people to agreement and smooth down the jagged edges of the possible into a workable finish.

The probabilizer's choice-making style is about maximizing the chances of getting results and reducing risk. But here is one of the potential shortcomings of this leadership bias: probabilizers may follow the path of least resistance, even when it is not the right course. They can be too risk-averse to strategize imaginatively and too concerned with the interests of others to implement their choices in the teeth of opposition. At worst, probabilizers can be mediocre leaders, mere time-servers who are afraid of making unpopular decisions and unable to make a difference.

Take the case of Theresa, a sophisticated and charming civil servant running a small Whitehall department. Working in a predominantly male-dominated environment, she had been effective in bringing people together and developing new policies. Yet she lacked confidence in her ability to expose the department's out-of-date procedures to new thinking and was becoming increasingly aware of her limitations, as far as implementing policy was concerned. 'I don't want to produce marvellous policy documents that are then filed and forgotten', she said.

In coaching, we started working on helping Theresa to organize strategic brainstorming sessions and opening up the decision-making process to others, especially some of the forward-looking people in the department who felt they had been ignored in the past. At the same time, we looked at what made it so difficult for Theresa to implement decisions. She revealed that it was the tough, uncompromising conversations with those who failed to action policies that were most problematic for her. Making strategic choices was consensual, which she enjoyed. When it comes to forcing through ideas, making actions happen and 'banging heads together,' she said, 'I feel I'm exposed, as though I were alone on a hillside.' In the end, learning to manage this feeling was probably the most important step in Theresa's progress towards becoming a more complete leader.

The leader as actualizer

The actualizing leader is all about action and results. This choice-making style is direct and to the point and can cut through long-winded corporate decision-making and false consensus-building. Actualizers can be highly effective in emergencies by 'getting down to it', whereas others may want to use time that is not really available. Actualizers are in their element when a strategy has been signed off and the priority is strictly about implementing it, especially in difficult circumstances.

The problem for this leadership style is that it can be too direct, too inimical for effective strategizing and too distancing of those who should be involved in good decision-making. It is a style dominated by imperatives, and it can miss out on the benefits of listening and questioning. Also actualizers may find ambiguity difficult, which can be a real drawback since leadership is steeped in ambiguity. They may try to ride roughshod over the complexities of a situation, promoting a potentially dangerous pseudo-certainty.

Consider Morris, a highly experienced engineer, who described himself as a 'no-nonsense doer' who was coming to the end of his first year as chief executive of an electricity supply company. He could be charismatic in his convictions but obstinate in his refusal to change his mind. His priority was always about 'getting things done', regardless of whose job description it fell under, which was alienating many of his department heads. One of them complained that Morris's abrasive, non-consultative style was 'de-skilling' many of the company's talented energy specialists and generally demoralizing the staff.

Early on in the coaching, Morris decided to commission research into the company's strategy and culture, even though he said he knew exactly what the outcome would be. In fact, the research suggested a new area of expansion in renewable energy that Morris had previously dismissed out of hand. Morris's willingness to acknowledge this opportunity, and to allow his specialists to lead it, took the company in a new, more productive direction. The research also suggested that the organization preferred a culture in which decision-making was 'firm and unfussy' but not dictatorial. In response, Morris began trying to establish a new personal dialectic for himself, walking a delicate line between the firm and the authoritarian. This, too, eventually bore fruit for him and his company.

Tough or nice: Another leadership dialectic

Another personality dimension that is highly relevant to coaching leadership is dominance and supportiveness. Leadership often attracts dominant executives who are strongly motivated by the desire for power. Some of these see the world of work as a binary choice between winners and losers. In consequence, they interpret colleagues as competitors rather than collaborators, an either–or stance that can make a 'give and take' approach feel like a defeat.

At the opposite pole, we find extremely supportive executives who may be highly competent but can struggle to achieve an effective attitude to power. Early in my coaching career, I was asked for a summary of executive coaching – in 10 words! 'Helping the nice get tougher and the tough get nicer' was the best I could come up with. Although it is a huge oversimplification, it does at least illustrate some key aspects of coaching around dominance and supportiveness. Often supportive leaders are simply too altruistic and too wary of individual power to achieve results. They may lack assertiveness and make choices based not on rights but on what is likely to be popular. In fact, their desire to give their followers what they want often means that their followers fail to get what they need. Coaching supportive executives is often aimed at enabling them to develop a framework for firm, consistent, fair decision-making that can turn their people-mindedness from a potential leadership weakness into a colossal strength.

Wanting to lead too much? The case of Lenny D. (continued from Chapter 1)

Lenny D., whom we first met at the beginning of the book, was definitely on the tough side of the tough–nice divide. He seemed almost impossibly driven, following a workaholic schedule that left him little time for anything outside his work. Sending emails at 3.00 a.m. was not uncommon for Lenny. He had been given his first CEO role in a troubled music company by the private equity firm that had acquired it, following a string of successful consultancy roles he had performed for them. He was known for his determination to do whatever it took to succeed, relentless attention to detail and a ruthless negotiating style. These were qualities that had served him well in the past but now, running a once revered company with a dwindling roster of talent, something else was needed. Lenny genuinely wanted to lead, and that was clear from our first meeting, 'I've had it with being the hired gun, leading is what I was born for', he said. The problem was that Lenny had little knowledge of the music industry and little time for listening to those who did. At his worst, he created an atmosphere of fear for his staff, in which those who opposed him were branded as 'enemies of the business'.

Coaching Lenny was not straightforward. Business coaches Ludeman and Erlandson (2004: 61) talk of the danger of 'playing it loose and light' when coaching 'alpha males', a broad category to be sure, but one in which Lenny would undoubtedly have included himself. Certainly, at times it was important for me to assert myself and even to try to force Lenny's choices. I asked him at one point: 'Do you really want to lead this company to success? If not, this coaching is pointless.' A look in his eyes suggested that he respected this kind of challenge. Similarly, when he began repeatedly rescheduling our sessions at the last minute, I countered by increasing my cancellation fee.

At the same time, the only way I really could help Lenny was by trying to enter into his reality and understanding how the world looked for him. Part of what drove him, he revealed, was a fierce need to be the best at everything. In the past, he had tried to divert some of his energy away from work towards leisure activities but whatever he did, whether it was playing squash or learning jazz dancing, he did with such fierce competitiveness that it offered little respite.

The real problem was that Lenny felt the need to prove himself at every turn. This need stemmed from a lack of confidence about who he really was. He traced this back to his mother, who had emigrated from Russia to the East End of London and brought him up on her own. She had been extremely ambitious for him, he said, 'trying to make up for all that she'd lost in her life, I guess'. Lenny described her attitude to him as 'relentlessly critical; she never let me get away with anything'. He explained how he had felt suffocated by this attitude. When I asked him how it might feel for his staff to be treated like this, it gave him pause for thought. As Lenny talked through his childhood, something more profound seemed to turn around, as he began to realize just how unflaggingly supportive his mother had been to him. This started him rethinking his need for domination.

The way forward for Lenny was to set himself completely new objectives. He needed to change his time frame from the short term to the longer term, which was a real shift for him but he managed to make it. He also realized that he had to stand up to his board and manage their expectations, while making a start on empowering his team. Lenny's leadership style slowly started to become more balanced, although there were still spectacular setbacks, as a succession of personal assistants walked out on him, unable to bear his 'control freak' ways. He made it his goal to retain his next PA, which he achieved, in part by experimenting with what was, for him, the novelty of apologizing. He also regularly monitored everything he said to her with a view to improvement. At the same time, he worked hard on his listening skills in order to understand more about the industry he was in. Crucially, he also gave more free rein to developing talent than he had been prepared to countenance previously, while stamping down on some of the artists' excessive expenditure. Lenny's struggle to balance dominance and supportiveness in his leadership style was ongoing but he undoubtedly achieved a better equilibrium through coaching. As a result, bit by bit, the fortunes of his company began to improve.

17

Coaching managerial expertise

Helping clients to develop their managerial expertise is another popular application of coaching. This may be appropriate when an executive lacks specific management skills or even all-round know-how. Such a situation is quite common in some areas of industry today, particularly in knowledge-based sectors where the main criterion for promotion is often specialist expertise rather than managerial aptitude. Executives may find themselves either managing others with little previous experience or in situations that are substantially more complex and demanding than situations where they have managed previously.

In interactional coaching it is impossible to cover all the skills that formal management training can address but a huge amount can be achieved by applying the choice focus to specific managerial tasks. Helping a manager go through the cycle of choice can identify the real choices involved in any particular managerial activity, as opposed to the mirage choices. This is often enough for him to get on with the job with a new sense of purpose.

In fact, there is an established tradition of placing choice-making at the core of management expertise. For example, in his highly influential account of what a manager's job consists of, Mintzberg (1990) suggests that four of a manager's ten basic roles are what he calls 'decisional'. The other roles, based on a manager's 'informational' and 'interpersonal' tasks, he also sees as implicated in decision-making. We have already looked at the influence of choice in many areas that are important for managerial expertise, such as strategizing and vision-making, self-knowledge, building interpersonal relationships and communication. In this chapter, I want to illustrate this connection further by reviewing how the choice focus can help the interactional coach to address other specific managerial skills, including time management, recruitment, delegation and remuneration.

Time management

Effective management, it might be said, is simply effective time management. It involves making the right choices about the past and the future, which enables the manager to select his priorities day to day. It is also about accepting the reality of a job. As Mintzberg (1990: 164) observes, 'folklore' may claim that a manager's job is scheduled, orderly and structured but the reality is that it is 'characterized by brevity, variety and discontinuity' and is subject to constant interruptions. The manager has to define the real choices that are available to him, as opposed to the illusory choices he feels he ought to be making. Using his interactional map to define the actual relationships between competing stakeholders – as opposed to their official status – can help him enormously in this. It is also crucial to differentiate what is important in the short term from what is important in the longer term. Only in this way can tough choices be made between what an executive might feel he would like to be doing in his job and what is absolutely essential to its success.

Recruitment

Recruitment is another important arena of managerial choice. Managers often spend a good deal of time and effort in attracting and selecting the right staff, often more than they realize. One coachee, a managing director of a health-care company that had a track record of high staff turnover, was amazed to find that she spent over 30% of her working time on recruitment issues. Coaching around this issue starts by applying the cardinal questions: What does the coachee want? How does a new hire relate to her business strategy? How do they need to fit in with her team and other interactors? The actualization stage of recruitment is the job interview, which is often one of the most intense workplace interactions for everyone concerned. Here an interviewing manager may go deep into her personal values and interactional assumptions. She probably has a good deal of information about the candidate in terms of qualifications and job experience but the real choices she has to make go beyond a CV. They are about who the candidate really is as a person and who they will become if they get the job.

Often choices that are made at this stage turn out to have a transformational effect, for good or for bad. I recall one client who reluctantly hired what she considered an extremely 'unpromising' candidate, who a few years later had become the bedrock of her department. Another coachee made an impulsive choice in appointing a sales executive and then spent a long time unsuccessfully trying to develop him for the role, followed by almost as much time painfully exiting him from the company, at considerable cost to his own reputation.

Motivation

Choice also plays a significant part in motivation. In fact, a manager has an array of options facing him about how to get the best out of her staff. These often involve delicate balances. Should she, for example, spend most of her time with her team members or represent them in other ways in the organization? Should she champion individual performance or build team spirit, or should she focus more on accomplishing tasks herself than on creating competence in her staff?

It is easy to get these balances wrong. Take the relationship between the nature of a job and the personality of the person who performs it. On the one hand, a job has a kind of objective existence, in terms of its description, terms and conditions and place in a network of other jobs. On the other hand, every successful job is performed by a person who is giving something unique to it. Indeed, from a motivational point of view, it is crucial that an employee feels that his job is subjectively fulfilling and that he is not just a cog in a machine.

Getting this balance right in coaching is usually about helping the coachee to gain a new perspective on the choices involved in a situation – which can sometimes reveal hidden expertise. Consider the case of Carmen, who was struggling to motivate Padraig, who she had hired six months earlier after a long, sophisticated selection process. I've just referred to the psychological intensity of the job interview but it is ironic just how quickly the penetrating questions and revealing scenarios explored in that context are forgotten, as though they had no ongoing relevance to the job. And yet, from a motivational viewpoint, it is hugely valuable for a manager to know who a direct report is and what he wants. So it was that after spending some time with Carmen, analysing her interactions with Padraig, she was amazed to realize how much she had become fixated on the technicalities of the job, rather than on the personality of person undertaking it. Once she revived the interest she had shown in Padraig in his job interview, before he had even joined the company, her ability to motivate him improved immensely.

Delegation

Delegation is another key managerial task that involves a manager's fundamental choices. A manager's deep-lying values and psychological preferences are often revealed by how he decides which work to delegate, to whom, on what basis and in which time frame. In part, delegation involves dealing with the anxiety of freedom, which in some measure stems from our awareness of the power of our choices. This was certainly the case with Rupert, a manager whose team seemed to be in conflict with itself and everyone else. Rupert had little respect for the freedom of his direct reports and found it intolerable if they made mistakes. So he over-managed them, depriving them of the ability to make any choices of their own. He then complained that his staff 'behaved like children', incapable of independent action. Perhaps this secretly satisfied Rupert because it seemed to assure him of his status, but ultimately it frustrated him because his staff constantly underperformed, which only entailed more managerial work for him. The way out of this cycle of mistrust was for Rupert to start using his own freedom as a manager more authentically, which meant starting to take ownership for his own anxiety and letting his team take more responsibility for their choices.

What the manager chooses to give to others, including those tasks she particularly enjoys or excels at, is part of the dialectic of renunciation and says something profound about who she is and what she wants. Simply articulating these choices in coaching, and following the dialogue to where it leads the client, may be enough to change her way of delegating.

Other areas of managerial expertise

There are many other aspects of managerial life that the choice focus can help to illuminate. For example, budgeting is fundamentally a process of deciding on priorities, on what can and can't be afforded, in which the interaction between gain and renunciation again plays an important role. The same can be said of managerial tasks such as developing an external marketing strategy, positioning the team within the organization, agreeing an advertising campaign, deciding on suppliers for IT and other equipment, and so on. In all of these areas, there is specific technical and local knowledge that needs to be mastered if the best choices are to be made. This is knowledge that the coach can help the coachee to organize for himself but cannot provide for him. At the same time, helping the coachee to identify the core dilemma involved in these managerial tasks and relating this to his ways of choosing may well turn out to be extremely helpful. In the end, self-knowledge can be the most telling form of knowledge.

Consider the role of remuneration, which can be a crucial factor in the success of a team, especially where managers have considerable leeway over individual levels of staff reward. Understanding a complex system of performance-related pay may be a pre-condition of good decision-making but key choices in this field are often less motivated by technical matters than by personal and interpersonal issues. Take the case of Bruce, a confident, fast-talking team manager in a commodity brokerage, who spent two sessions with me trying to decide which of two direct reports he should award an annual bonus. One was a lively, innovative newcomer to the team, the other a long-serving stalwart who had made substantial sacrifices to help out the team in a crisis. Bruce had tried to persuade his manager to split the bonus between the two of them but was compelled to choose one or the other. This was made more difficult by the possibility that whoever lost out on the bonus might leave the company, as both were very marketable executives. In the final analysis, Bruce decided to reward the long-serving team member, even though he had none of the brilliance of the newcomer. Bruce was genuinely surprised by his decision – up to this point he would have said his management philosophy was 'hire the best, fire the rest' – but once he had located the place of team loyalty in his new hierarchy of values the choice was easy.

As Bruce's case illustrates, the aim of coaching managerial expertise is not to train coachees as managers but to focus them on what is most important in their role and thus promote clarity around their choice-making and enhance their optative awareness. If the coach has managerial experience, this can also help in coaching this purpose, as it provides another source of insight. As for psychologically trained coaches who lack practical management experience, it seems not unreasonable that they should devote a portion of their continuing development to studying management and leadership skills, just as business coaches may be expected to devote some of their time to the study of psychology.

Part 7

Other coaching purposes

18

Coaching creativity and innovation

Innovation is at the forefront of the contemporary executive's concerns. In the industrialized world it seems that continued creativity is almost a condition for survival, and yet innovation is one of the most demanding forms of choice-making. It involves an assault on the unknown and a defiance of uncertainty in the unstructured realm of possibility. It is an assertion of the importance of play, an activity in which, as Sartre (1958: 580) reminds us, we make our own rules as we go along, resisting the 'spirit of seriousness'. But the temptation is often to run for the sanctuary of structure as soon as possible. This shift may be prompted by a recognition of how challenging it is to turn even the best ideas into workable products and services in the real world, but if conducted too soon it is a move that can destroy authentic inspiration.

That is why in coaching creativity it really pays off to acknowledge the three stages of the choice cycle, as each phase of innovation makes very different demands. In this chapter, we'll also see that this coaching purpose involves recognizing the fact that different individuals exhibit very different attitudes to, and aptitudes for, creativity. This doesn't mean that some people are creative and others are not, but that an individual's capacity for innovation is much more complex than an undifferentiated 'one size fits all' attitude to creativity allows for. The ISO distinction between originators and accommodators can help to identify the client's particular type of creativity. Nor is innovation in organizations simply an individual pursuit. For managers of innovation, creating a culture of creativity can also be a major challenge, as we'll observe.

The stages of creativity

All three stages of the choice cycle are important for coaching creativity but it is at the first, possibilizing, stage that the challenges and opportunities of innovation are most intense. Working in the domain of the possible means working with the freedom of the unknown to develop strategies or ideas that may have never existed before. For many clients, staying in the delta of the possible is difficult; there is an urge to move quickly to more probable and actual choices. 'There's no such thing as a bad idea' is the mantra for this creative zone, but putting this into practice is easier said than done. Often a client will respond to his own ideas with practical considerations, such as:

> There's no budget for that . . . it's too much like something that already exists . . . it will take too long to develop . . . I'll never get approval . . . it crosses into a colleague's territory . . .

This kind of objection is perfectly legitimate at the probabilizing stage of innovation but it can be destructive during possibilization. It tends to shut down the kind of imaginative freedom that leads to new ways of thinking, working and doing. At the same time, the act of possibilizing can seem abstract and arid to some clients, while for others it is a struggle to go beyond the known universe of a product and service, with which they may be acquainted in microscopic detail. So how can we brainstorm new ideas in a way that helps the client to transcend his known choices?

One technique that can be used to facilitate brainstorming in coaching is 'triggered connections'. To do this, take a trigger word, preferably one that is concrete and rich in meaning, and ask the client to come up with connections to the target object. So imagine we are trying to develop ideas for a new mobile phone and we take 'fox' as the trigger word. The client might come up with the following connections: a phone that is an usual colour like a fox (i.e. russet red) or a phone that, like a fox, goes to ground (i.e. one that can be colour coordinated, camouflaged or hidden in clothing). Or what about a phone that scavenges in the manner of an urban fox – one that can be charged from all sorts of other appliances? 'Cunning as a fox' is a phrase that might intrigue the client, leading to the idea of a phone that has more functionality, such as a smartphone. In this way, clients can be helped to exploit the creative richness of possibilizing.

Help may also be needed at the selection and implementation stages of the choice cycle. Turning free-floating, creative ideas into probabilities, let alone actualities, is also a considerable challenge. The practical demands of a product or the conventions of genre cannot simply be ignored. Accommodators, who tend to be conventional and structured in their thinking, often come into their own at these practical phases of innovation, where originators may start to flounder, get bored or simply move on to the next possibilization.

The interactional self and creativity

Creativity at work involves finding the right personal dialectic in relation to the dimensions of the interactional self. What can make innovation so precious – its distance from the status quo – can also make it challenging when it comes to interpersonal relationships. Standing out from the crowd may be pressurizing but being intimated by others or compromising too readily can reduce your creativity. On the other hand, ignoring a client's brief and focusing only on what is personally stimulating is also likely to be problematic, so the key is to find your own creative point of balance.

Time can also be a paradoxical factor in innovation. For instance, innovation can take a long time and require extraordinary patience. Many an invention or innovative working practice has gone by the board due to the frustration of constant delays. Yet too much time can also be a drain on creativity. Often there is nothing like an imminent deadline to bring out the best in creative thinking. For instance, some years ago, many months of intensive research and development at BBC television failed to produce a viable outline for an ambitious new soap opera. In the end a 40-minute deadline was enough to produce the basic format of what turned out to be one of most successful TV serial dramas ever: *EastEnders* (Smith and Holland, 1987).

Coaching highly creative people often involves working with aspects of the interactional self. Originators, for example, often have difficulties with the interpersonal implications of creativity, which the open, non-competitive environment of coaching can help them get around. Take Chloe, a young web designer who had made a name for herself through her strikingly original designs. In spite of her success, she was finding it increasingly difficult to fit into her working environment. She said that people thought she was 'weird'. Normally that didn't disturb her, as she said she had grown up with that accusation, but now she was beginning to feel like 'an alien' and it was affecting her work. She said she found herself censoring designs that came to her spontaneously and substituting them for ideas that she thought would meet the approval of others, even though she had the authority to sign off on her own designs. It turned out that the solution for Chloe was not to compromise on her graphic designs but to work much harder on her social skills, trying to interest herself in her colleagues rather than staying aloof from them. In this way, she made her working environment more amenable without having to sacrifice her creative originality.

Ben C. and the blame culture of creativity

Another challenge for creative individuals consists of taking a step up in an organization and managing the creativity of others. This can involve quite a radical switching of perspectives from self to others. Ben C., a recently appointed head of production in a UK-based television company, couldn't understand why his producers were failing to come up with original programme ideas. As a New Yorker whose career had been developed in the tough television environment of his home town, he also kept asking: 'Why do our best ideas never seem to get developed?'

When I asked Ben how he normally went about producing new programme ideas, he replied:

> I'm used to getting twenty people around a desk to fight for the next big idea. If you haven't got the cajones to speak up, forget it! You won't be asked back a second time.

We looked at how appropriate this format was for his relatively inexperienced UK production team, who were more used to a 'soft sell' approach to creativity rather than this 'hard sell' attitude. Ben began to acknowledge that there could be a problem here and started to look at less confrontational methods of creative development. His very expressive way of talking also stood out. He could be amusing and inspirational but also intimidating in his directness. Exploring some of the negative effects of this communication style on his staff helped him to develop alternative ways of talking to them.

Perhaps the biggest thing Ben needed to change was his tendency to heap opprobrium on anyone who fell short of his high standards. He not only seemed to exemplify this blame culture but felt it was the only true spur to creativity. And yet he recognized that creativity involved making mistakes and he could be engagingly frank about some of his own 'career disasters'. He seemed to espouse a double imperative: 'Be original, take risks but don't fail!' In this, Ben was simply rehearsing a contradiction about innovation that many organizations fall into. The result was that Ben's producers were so concerned about making mistakes that they opted for the safest or most conventional programme ideas. This, of course, only exacerbated Ben's criticism of them. Once he started to examine this deeply embedded double standard, he was able to modify his behaviour in relation to it and his management of creativity changed for the better.

Coaching accommodators

What about coaching less obviously creative people? First of all, it is important to realize that people who see themselves as accommodators rather than originators are not incapable of original ideas. It is just that they are less inclined to challenge themselves to be original and more prone to dismiss new ideas as impractical. Originators tend to question the status quo as a matter of course, asking: 'Why can't we do this better or at least differently?' Accommodators are more likely to say: 'If it ain't broke why fix it?' But accommodators are more than able to enter into the dialectic between the known and the unknown when new solutions have to be found. Sometimes, it is the task of coaching to encourage this interaction, perhaps by helping a client stay within the possibilizing zone and refrain from final choices for longer than normal.

Antonia is an example of an accommodator who changed her creative style through coaching. She was a banker, whose career had been built on meticulous attention to detail and dependability in producing evidence-based solutions for her commercial customers. She played by the rules and stuck to the tried and tested forms of lending. But her bank was changing fast, introducing fewer standardized, 'vanilla' products and focusing on more complex solutions, often uniquely tailored for individual customers. She was finding this transition extremely arduous, as she was deeply sceptical about new methods and wary of innovation.

Antonia objected to new products on the grounds that they often did not get approval by the industry regulator and so wasted a good deal of time. We started examining 'the statistics of innovation' in her field and it became clear that for every successful new product there were dozens, perhaps hundreds, that fail. She concluded – if a shade reluctantly – that only by working on numerous product ideas was there any chance of coming up with a winner. She also began to realize that her dismissal of the modernizers in her department – she called them 'rude, unrealistic, pie-in-the-sky thinkers' – put her in a very exposed career position that did not reflect her real emotional commitment to her bank. And she was quite shocked when she became aware of the sneering expression that appeared on her face when she spoke about new products and how this could antagonize people in a way she did not intend. Trying to be more open-minded and receptive to new suggestions put Antonia on a far more productive track. She began to combine her scepticism with a perceptive openness to what was workable in new product ideas, a combination that eventually enabled her to transform her common sense into an asset rather than a hindrance.

Rediscovering creativity

Finally, it is important to note that creativity sometimes comes as a revelation. One of the enemies of innovation is routine, the constant need to make ends fit means, which can prevent us from seeing the originality of our own choices. Embedded assumptions and stereotypes about creativity can easily blind us to real innovation. Take the case of Justin, a senior civil servant who was known and respected for his diplomacy and ability to bring diverse viewpoints together and produce practicable solutions. Working in a highly volatile department, headed by an even more volatile Minister of State, he was surrounded by competing egos and chaotic policy-making. 'Just getting through a week without the whole thing blowing up in your face is a minor miracle', he sighed. What caused him most concern personally and professionally was his belief that, in dealing with day-to-day contingencies, his own innovativeness had been diminished. He saw colleagues in other departments as bold trail-blazers and creative modernizers but he saw himself as increasingly unimaginative and routine-bound.

So when Justin's ISO responses suggested that he was an originator, he was pleasantly surprised. As we explored how he went about bringing people together in his department, his real creativity started to reveal itself. It seemed that he was constantly possibilizing, bringing unexpected and sometimes very novel solutions to practical problems. He was seen as the ultimate probabilizer – discreet, smooth and quietly effective – but in reality he was offering a stream of imaginative ideas and original options.

In part, Justin's problem was that he had started to believe his own reputation, even going along with the notion that his colleagues were the ones who were coming up with the best solutions. In fact, one of Justin's most successful ploys was to drop a novel suggestion into a meeting with such subtly that nobody noticed it, until it miraculously resurfaced some time later, now presented as somebody else's idea. It was as though Justin had been deceived by his own subtlety. Once he started to reinterpret the nature of his contribution at work, he began to appreciate his unique style of creativity and thus felt much more comfortable about himself.

19

Coaching stress: Reclaiming the power of choice

Stress is ubiquitous in coaching. It comes in many guises: as a dramatic, one-off appearance, as a theme that weaves in and out of a coaching series or as the initiating purpose of an entire assignment. Whatever its form, the real issues provoking the stress may turn out to be almost anything within the coachee's world. For this very reason, the experience of stress, however challenging, can be valuable as an instrument of learning. It is often an indicator of what really matters to a person and reveals the fundamental choices she is making.

Stress and owning your anxiety

Stress is linked to anxiety, which is never too far away from human reality. From the interactional point of view, anxiety is a form of choice consciousness. Because we have choices, we can always see that things could be different, especially in the future, and that they could be worse as well as better. Anxiety is the price we pay for our freedom of choice; it is 'the dizziness of freedom', to recall Kierkegaard's (1980: 61) memorable phrase. Often, extreme emotions are a result of trying to get rid of anxiety by blaming it on others or using them as a pretext for expressing pent-up feelings. Interactional coaching aims to help clients stop disowning their anxiety and so be in a better position to take responsibility for themselves. In so doing, they move towards what Emmy van Deurzen-Smith calls 'authentic living', which implies 'a resolute choice about what is one's own and what is not' (1988: 54).

If choice is at the heart of anxiety, it is the apparent disappearance of choice that marks out stress. Anxiety is about our awareness of what we are capable of doing and, as such, is quite different from fear. As Sartre suggests: 'Fear is fear of being in the world, anxiety is anxiety before myself' (1958: 28). Stress seems to be somewhere in between, 'a halfway station on the way to anxiety', as May (1977: 113) calls it, in which there is pressure, uncertainty and a strong sense of the negative consequences awaiting an action. At worst, it is an experience of being charged with an impossible task that you are incapable of performing adequately, yet for which you will ultimately be held responsible. When the experience of stress reaches a crescendo it can be very disturbing, bringing not only psychological distress but also a range of physical symptoms, such as headaches, insomnia and panic attacks (Cooper et al., 1988).

Feeling 'choiceless'

'I have no choice . . . I feel powerless', said one client, locked into an ambitious project he seemed to have no control over. Often we feel so committed to our goals – and to our designs on the future – that we become captive to them. In this situation we forget we always have choices, as expressed in the concept of categorical choice that I outlined in Chapter 1. Stress coaching is about helping the client to restore the reality of choice.

Reasserting control over this situation has to start with the coachee's realization of the choices he is actually making. This can be seen as stepping back, a process of helping the client to distance himself from the intensity of his predicament. From this position, it is possible to get a glimpse of the aims, expectations and intentions he is taking for granted. Even physical measures, such as deep breathing, can help us to escape the clutches of these embedded choices. So too can sport or other leisure activities, which throw us into a world of quite different rules, challenges and emotions, a paradigm shift that can be very effective in relieving stress.

Changing your choices means setting new priorities, especially when your old goals have become warped and distorted. This was the situation Sian found herself in, when covering for a colleague who was on sick leave. Sian was an extremely conscientious computer programmer who was determined not to let anyone down, but when we started identifying her goals it seemed she was trying to go in two opposite directions at once. She said, 'I reckon my normal job takes up 125% of my time', and calculated that her absent colleague's workload was similar. 'So now you're trying to deliver 250% of your job?', I asked her. In effect, Sian was making a mirage choice to perform a second job with the same total commitment and efficiency she brought to her own role. That is not to say that she didn't believe in this mirage – the whole point of an illusion is that we believe it is true – but the inner contradictions of this choice increasingly expressed themselves in physical symptoms of stress. Once she realized this, she was able to scale down her commitment to her covering role quite radically and fortify herself against any unjustified criticism on this score. After that, her basically sensible attitude to life returned and her stress symptoms began to disappear.

Stress coaching involves managing time. There is no clearer evidence of the magnetic pull of the future than the lived experience of someone anticipating a high-pressure event. Often this has an unsettling effect on all sorts of unrelated day-to-day activities. One way of dealing with this corrosive uncertainty is by trying to impose structure on it by means of deadlines. But these decisions sometimes turn out to be more oppressive in their effect than the choices they are intended to manage. Being rushed into decisions that you have no time to consider properly can be deeply stressful. Helping the client to set a new time frame – a more realistic deadline, for example – is often an effective way of managing stress. In some cases, an even better solution for the client is to let things happen 'in their own good time'.

Stress and the choice cycle

In one sense, stress is a victory for the negative over positive in the dialectic that is constantly operating in our lives. Stress equals pressure added to uncertainty plus the possibility of a negative outcome. This is quite different from the lived experience of a pressurized, uncertain situation, from which a positive outcome is expected. At its most extreme, stress can be seen as a process of possibilizing that bypasses probabilizing and moves straight to imagined actuality. This electric charge of negative possibilities assumes the status of action and indeed seems to be interpreted by the central nervous system as such, as it triggers the physical symptoms of stress even though the precipitating 'danger' may only exist in the imagination of the individual.

This is why probabilizing can be an ideal antidote to stress. Simply asking the client to identify the probability of a stressful event occurring can help to restore a proper perspective. The chances of a catastrophic event such as an audience walking out of a presentation, for example, are extremely remote and yet this kind of image often looms large in our anticipation of an important speech. A steady, sober look at the choices really facing a client often has the desired effect of moving from a wildly possibilized state, where anything can happen, to a more probable state of affairs. This enables the client to see what his best possible choices are, however challenging they may be.

Sometimes, the whole of the choice cycle needs to be invoked. For instance, in the middle of a session, Barry, a successful entrepreneur, became very stressed about his new start-up venture. The transformation was striking. In general he was a model of composed enthusiasm, but suddenly his breathing became distressed, his face pale and he blurted out that he was experiencing panic attacks in the middle of the night. I asked him to remind me of the goals of the project and the probabilities surrounding its success. Barry began to list the great opportunity the venture presented, his own expertise and the previous experience and qualifications of his team. After a while, he concluded: 'If I fail it's because the idea isn't right or the time isn't right, not because I've neglected to do anything that I should have done.' With that, his normal breathing gradually resumed and his composed demeanour returned.

Stress and the sub-reflective level of consciousness

Finally, it is worth pointing out that stress is a subject where choice-focused learning would appear to meet contemporary psychobiology. Stress has been studied empirically in biological terms as a 'fight or flight' response that may be hard-wired into our evolutionary make-up (Cannon, 1931). Major physical changes occur, such as the release of hormones like cortisone, or other alterations in bodily functioning such as increased heart rate and redirected circulation of the blood (Green, 1994). These are prompted by the need for increased energy to respond to an imminent danger. All this would appear to occur at a neurological, sub-reflective level beyond the reach of conscious enquiry. Yet the stress response is clearly an interpretation of the world, because no actual danger needs to be present for it to occur and as such it must be considered as a kind of decision-making process. We know this because reflecting on it can bring it into consciousness and so enable us to change our choices. In phenomenological terms, we are simply dealing with another area of experience in which the person encounters the world, in his capacity as a 'body-subject' (Merleau-Ponty, 1962). This suggests that understanding choice is undoubtedly a central factor in effective stress management, whatever the theoretical language used to describe it.

20

Coaching 'failure', relapse and renewal

Many clients achieve what they want in coaching but it would be wrong to pretend that every coaching assignment delivers exactly the objectives that the client or her organization desires. The cycle of achievement doesn't always complete itself. Inevitably the coach and coachee will sometimes find themselves in situations where the coachee has not achieved what he wants and a next step is called for. In this chapter we explore the options before the coach and coachee in such circumstances, including trying again, re-probabilizing, re-possibilizing and promoting renewal. We'll also examine the idea of 'the Pyrrhic defeat', a paradoxical coaching situation that at first sight looks like failure but may turn out to be success in another guise.

The ambiguity of failure

In one sense, failure is a dramatic negation. At worst, the defeat of one's goals can be experienced as a severe psychological blow, a reduction to a powerless state that Laing (1960) compares to being 'petrified' or turned to stone. It can be hard to recover from this kind of failure. 'It was crushing,' said Kenneth about losing a long and bitter battle with competitors for a client contract, 'for months afterwards I felt almost paralysed when I saw any reference to the deal.' For a while, Kenneth chose to retreat from competitive situations, in the hope that if he gave up the chance of winning he would reduce the possibility of losing. This threatened to be a more expensive choice than he had at first thought, as his career started spiralling downwards. Only at this point was he able to pull himself back from the brink. It is a reminder that how we interpret our feelings about defeat often determines our ability to recover from it. In coaching failure, what a client makes of a negative event is always far more important than the nature of the event itself.

Yet, from another perspective, failure can be seen as something of an illusion. Existential thinkers take an unconventional view of failure, seeing it as the unavoidable partner of success. Famously Camus (1955) uses the Greek myth of Sisyphus as a symbol for the inevitable ups and downs of existence. As soon as Sisyphus pushes his boulder to the top of the mountain, it starts to roll down, and he has to begin his task all over again. This might seem a gloomy message but it dramatizes the important truth that, even at the very moment of achievement, success is fragile. It is never guaranteed but must be renewed and reinvigorated constantly.

Examining the experimentation that is at the core of empirical science is another way of putting failure into perspective. The process of 'trial and error' is about the interaction between two real states, not just a euphemism for 'delayed achievement'. In fact, there is a good deal more 'error' than 'trial' in the history of many a scientific discovery or technological breakthrough. Experiments that fail can be as rich in information as the ones that succeed. This is useful for the coach and the coachee to bear in mind when something seems to go wrong in the coaching process.

Try, try and try again

One of the most obvious responses to the coachee's failure to implement a strategy is to give it another go. Sometimes stepping back and analysing, in the cold light of day, what went wrong suggests that the client's original goals remain valid. It may have been sheer bad luck that caused an action to misfire, or a nuanced mistake rather than a dramatic error. For example, Ray presented a proposal to a customer that drew just a little too heavily on their close and long-standing relationship and not quite enough on his professionalism.

Although the customer may have been inclined to accept the deal, Ray had not given her enough to justify it to her board. Once he realized this, Ray presented the proposal again, this time more thoroughly and with due consideration for the customer's situation.

Time is a powerful resource when it comes to trying again. 'Failing once is an embarrassment, failing twice would be a disaster', one coachee said after a botched attempt to install a brilliant protégé in a new marketing function. But six months later, when the market conditions in his industry had changed considerably, his proposal went through unopposed. Sooner or later the choice landscape always changes, one way or the other. And we should never underestimate the role of a person's attitude to the future in arbitrating between success and failure. Executives who persist in their determination to initiate a project or win new business tend to outperform less perseverant rivals, even though this may mean enduring months, or even years, of setbacks.

Relapse and renewal

After a period of successful change, it is not uncommon for people to experience a form of relapse. There can be many reasons for this. Perhaps the client has not fully embraced his new way of making choices or maybe he has started to regard his success as guaranteed. Regarding achievement as a thing, acquired once and for all, like a certificate on the wall or a trophy in a cabinet, is asking for trouble. Sometimes a client becomes too fixed in the implementation stage of the choice cycle, where a predominantly closed attitude is necessary, and fails to open up to the new possibilities that are often essential if achievement is to be sustained. An executive may even profess to be bored with his success, although in my experience 'boredom' is rarely what it seems.

Several of these factors played a part in Vicky's struggle to sustain the positive changes she had made in a series of training courses. A radio producer, she seemed to have survived the crisis caused by her editor's threat to move her out of production unless she stopped 'winding up people and getting their backs up'. But her new style of choosing had not become embedded. Her old, abrasive way of interacting with others was returning and so were the complaints from her colleagues.

'Done that, been there', was Vicky's response to her training, She explained to me that her excitement about changing her interactional style had given way to boredom. 'I get impatient,' she said, 'it's hard to be forever thinking about what people might want. I just want to get on with the job.' It was Vicky's use of psychological language in an angry and blaming way that was striking. She talked about colleagues 'wanting too much validation from me' or needing to 'cut out the parent–child role'. She seemed to retain some of the terminology she had learned in her training but not its real meaning.

As we explored what was going on for Vicky, something fundamental seemed to emerge. What appeared to be pushing her back into her old ways was her fear that she would not be able to maintain her new, more open relationships. 'I had a burst of energy and the confidence to really make an effort,' she said, 'but I can't see myself getting that back.' In fact, her boredom and harsh criticism of her colleagues masked this profound self-doubt. We started looking at her key inter-actions, assessing the very real progress she had made in many cases. She admitted that she had to start winning over people again and she made a determined effort to listen attentively once more. Relatively quickly, she began redis-covering the relationships she had started to build. The doubts that had dramatically caused her to conclude that she could not change were gradually overcome and she began to become conscious of her choice-making at a deeper level. To me, this optative awareness suggested that Vicky was much more likely to maintain her progress this time.

'Re-probabilizing': Looking at other options

If a client's action plan really has failed, it may be worth going back to the probabilizing stage to see if another course of action would work better. Perhaps the client has a parallel choice strategy, in which case now is the time to put plan B or plan C into action. Here the goal remains the same but the path taken to reach it now changes. For instance, having failed to gain new resources by subtle persuasion, Alison threatened to resign if she wasn't given the extra staff she desperately needed. Her all-or-nothing strategy proved successful, perhaps because it was clear to her management that she genuinely meant it. Another client who failed to win over a reluctant team by trying to appeal to everyone in the team successfully switched to a strategy of going all out to change the mind of the most influential members of the group.

Reviewing the interactional map can also produce dividends. It is worth asking if the client's web of influence in the organization has changed in such a way as to interfere with the original plan or whether other interactors have emerged who might be useful. One client changed tactics after realizing that his access to the chief executive was being blocked by the very team he had chosen to commit himself to. Switching his allegiance to a rival team changed the political dynamics at the top of the company and brought about his desired result.

'Re-possibilizing': Starting the choice cycle again

Sometimes, a more radical response to failure is necessary, which entails returning to the choice identification stage and 're-possibilizing'. It may be that the client doesn't really want what she thinks she wants. Perhaps she cannot really see the future she is aiming at or perhaps something from the past is holding her back that she has not identified. One client confessed that she realized that she feared success late in her career because she thought it would make her regret all the time she had wasted when she was 'young enough to enjoy it'.

It may be a question of looking at the personal dimension of the self again. A previously undetected clash of values may be preventing the coachee from fully engaging with his chosen course of action. Although he tried to actualize his strategy, he was perhaps never doing more than going though the motions and so failure was more or less inevitable. Self-analysis is always useful for understanding precisely what went wrong in an intended action. Taking the client through this, step by step, may bring new insights.

Often the choice facing the coachee at this stage is stark: improve your ability to put your strategy into practice or change strategy altogether. Some clients may not be prepared to change their ambition or 'downgrade' their goals. 'I prefer honourable defeat to compromise', one client told me. But for others, re-possibilizing to a more attainable target represents a viable option for success.

A case in point is Moira's attempt to change the relationship between her human resources function and the business units it served. First time round, the initiative had ended in an uncomfortable mixture of misunderstanding and downright hostility on the part of the business. There seemed to be little chance for Moira to revive her initiative in its original form and she herself was smarting from the criticism she had received. But in coaching she managed to keep her focus on what could still be achieved in the situation and was refreshingly honest about the project and her own contribution to its failure. She soon came up with an alternative plan that was more modest in its scope than her first project. But by being prepared to climb down on her most controversial proposals and work tremendously hard with her two most powerful heads of business she managed to gain some respect for her plans. Over the following year – a much longer period than she had initially envisaged – she managed to turn this breathing space into a platform for a series of changes that went a good way to fulfilling her original objectives.

When failure turns out to be success: The case of Ricky W.

On occasion the changes of direction involved in coaching can be dramatic, so much so that, from some perspectives, the coaching assignment may look like a failure. Oppositional logic is at its most potent in what we can call 'the Pyrrhic defeat'. Just as Pyrrhus' victory was potentially illusory, so in coaching certain types of apparent failure may turn out to be simply another kind of success. We have already seen one form of the Pyrrhic defeat in the impasse or holding pattern in Chapter 10. Here the client is placed in a perfect balance between interacting forces, which does not result in immediate satisfaction but may lead to positive changes in time. Sometimes, however, this testimony to the ambiguity of failure can be more spectacular, leading to a radical revision of the client's ambitions at work. This may turn out to be a Damascene moment for the coachee, as the following case demonstrates, even if it can lead to some difficult conversations with the coaching sponsor.

Ricky W., the creative director of an advertising agency, was under pressure to raise his team's performance following a run of lost client pitches. Patricia, his forceful boss, had insisted that Ricky engage in coaching in order to turn around his losing streak. Over our first two sessions, I learned that Ricky was a highly creative individual with wide-ranging talents. He was a musician and a maker of short films, as well as an outstanding graphic artist and visualizer. More unusually perhaps for someone who seemed so at home in the ultra-urban world of a Soho media company, he was also a lover of the great outdoors. He was a keen sailor with a passion for adventurous journeys, which called for practicality and self-reliance. I got the sense of a man who could have done any number of different careers and been successful at them, and yet there was no question of his commitment to his current role, as far as I could see. He told me: 'I'm prepared to learn anything I have to in order to make this a success, for me and my team.'

It quickly became apparent that it was Ricky's combination of high creativity and independence that was inhibiting his team's performance. He kept coming up with original and innovative ideas but without due consideration for what the client wanted. As a consequence, he was losing out to less creative but more market-focused pitches by rival companies. He also took too much of the responsibility for originating ideas and had a tendency to skirt over rejections rather than seeing what could be learned from them. This was demoralizing the team and reducing their effectiveness.

Over the next six sessions, Ricky looked long and hard at his interactions with himself and others and began to change his management practices. He started to develop a more intense client-focus, less of a 'head in the clouds' approach, as he called it, and began to make better use of the creative talents of his team. The results started to come, with a couple of small wins. Then, quite out of the blue, a major client dismissed its existing agency and, at very short notice, invited a range of agencies to pitch for its entire business. Ricky's team won what turned out to be a huge contract. This totally transformed Ricky's standing with Patricia and with his team.

It was something of a shock, therefore, when Ricky announced during our last session that the change brought about by coaching was not what it had seemed – at least to me. He was very appreciative of our work together and said he had learned more about creative management in the past few months than in his entire career. 'But for me,' he went on, 'this whole process has made me think about what I really want to do – and it's not this any more.' He declared that he intended to move from London to the south coast, put all his savings into buying an ocean-going yacht and earn his living by chartering it to others. 'The rest of the time,' he said, 'I'm going to be sailing around the world.'

I wasn't totally surprised by his choice – I could see how it related to his values – but I knew it would not be popular in the organization. Patricia was furious at the news and, having congratulated me warmly a few weeks earlier on 'turning around Ricky', she now called me in to interrogate me about what had 'really been going on' in the coaching sessions. Clearly, what seemed like success to Ricky – a great turning point in his life, in fact – looked like rank failure to his boss. I told Patricia that this turn of events had come as a surprise to me too but added that 'when someone really finds what they want and has the courage to pursue it, it can be inspiring for everyone'. For the first time, Patricia's expression seemed to brighten up. 'Good line,' she said, 'I can use that to explain to Ricky's clients why he won't be around any more!'

The wrong kind of success may be the exception rather than the rule in coaching, but it is an almost inevitable by-product of an organization's desire to bring out the best possible performance from its employees. Executives who are not doing what they want are unlikely to be at the top of their game, and sometimes it is only by going through the choice cycle that they discover what they really do want. Reality always delivers; it just doesn't always deliver what we expect it to deliver.

Inevitably, coaching is judged in terms of its outcomes but these are never wholly predictable and are not always the best criteria for evaluating the real worth of a coaching assignment. As Kierkegaard (1992: 485) emphasized, 'in choice it is less a matter of choosing correctly than the energy, earnest and feeling with which one chooses'. If coaching addresses the real issues in the right way and advances the coachee's ability to recognize and take responsibility for his own choices, the final outcome is always likely to be a success, whatever its superficial appearance.

Conclusion

The interactional coach

What does it take to coach interactionally? The short answer is: the ability to help a client to find and implement his optimal choices in the specific situation in which he finds himself. This in turn requires the coach to make his own optimal choices in the coaching relationship. Other qualifications for the interactional coach that we'll examine in this chapter include embracing the oppositional logic of coaching, having the ability to evaluate a coaching assignment and being comfortable in all the aspects of the choice cycle and the interactional self. We'll also look at the basic competences of executive coaching from an interactional viewpoint and the quality of the coach's commitment to the coachee.

The oppositional logic of coaching

As I suggested in the first chapter of this book, coaching in some ways is a profession pervaded by oppositional logic. It is an occupation that facilitates learning but really aims to develop a client's ability to learn, rather than any specific skill set. It endeavours to help clients make the best of their situations and yet does so most successfully by helping them to realize that they are the ultimate experts in their situations. It is an activity that puts an intense spotlight on the coachee but it is the coaching relationship that often brings about actual change.

Another paradox of the profession is that clients are often at least as impressed by what a coach did before he or she became a coach than by his or her specific coaching expertise. One can't imagine this response to a doctor or a lawyer! But this attitude does at least underline the importance of work experience for coaching, even if, as Bluckert (2006) points out, coaches with impressive business credentials or success at sport sometimes have the reputation to attract clients but not necessarily the ability to coach them. This is why a combination of business experience and psychological training can be so useful in helping coaches to acquire the basic skills of their trade.

One of the most important preconditions for coaching is that the coach must want to coach. Even this is not as self-evident as it seems, because for some people – especially those with a strong orientation towards action – the prospect of spending most of their working lives listening to others is far from appealing. At the same time, the desire to coach needs to be translated into a desire for the coachee to realize his optimal choices at work. This doesn't mean that the coach wants nothing, but that what he wants is directed at the client's world to a greater extent than in many professional roles.

How do you know you are doing a good job?

Several types of evaluation are used by the interactional coach to assess the effectiveness of a coaching assignment, depending on the contracted agreement with the coachee and the coaching sponsor. In some cases the evaluation may be formal, perhaps consisting of 360-degree feedback before and after the coaching series; in other cases a more informal consultation with the coaching sponsor may suffice. Sometimes, evaluation simply consists of the conclusions reached by coach and coachee in their final session.

When, as a coach, do you get a sense of doing a good job during a coaching assignment? Sometimes, this realization comes when a client deliberately reflects on changes in his behaviour. For example, a coachee might state: 'In the past I would have said I know exactly how that new initiative will turn out but now I'm more open-minded about it.' Or perhaps the change in behaviour is communicated unconsciously by the client, through a more relaxed facial expression or a more assertive body posture. Often a positive change occurs in the interval between sessions, as we've seen several times in this book, when a client reports something that suggests she is achieving her coaching goals. Or perhaps the coach observes something in a coachee's description of events that the coachee doesn't notice but that also seems to confirm that a process of change is under way.

The coach's personal dimension: Developing optative awareness

The reader won't be surprised to hear that the evaluating process and every other aspect of the coach's role are bound up with the dimensions of the interactional self. Just as the coachee is encouraged to work in the dimensions of time, self and others, so the coach needs to monitor his thoughts, feelings and actions in these terms.

Let's start with the self dimension. Throughout the coaching process, the coach's optative awareness – his consciousness of the choices he is making during the coach processes and the responsibility he takes for them – plays a major role. This ability to analyse one's own choices and desires is also important in order to stay with the uncertainty that the self-structuring nature of coaching often provokes. Often the most revealing thoughts are the most difficult, such as the feeling that you don't understand a client or don't trust her, or some element of guilt or conflict. These interpretations need to be brought to a reflective level. There is no escaping choice for the coach any more than for the coachee, but using choice deferral and the other techniques of expert listening that I outlined in Chapter 3 can help to make the coach's choices as informed as possible. Indeed, practising open listening on oneself is one of the coach's most powerful tools.

This is particularly important in helping the client to find the right techniques and skills to develop and implement his strategy. There is a dialectic between the descriptive and the prescriptive, which inevitably plays in and out of the coaching process. There are no guarantees that the coach makes the right choices in offering skills coaching, for example, or particular ideas or models or even self-disclosure, except that these are made in the spirit of offering, fully recognizing the client's freedom to choose.

A useful self-monitoring question for the interactional coach is: 'What part am I playing in the client's choice-making?' If the answer is 'none at all', there may be a question as to the value of the coaching; if the response is 'a good deal', it may be that the coach is taking too strong a role in directing or guiding the coachee. Somewhere between these two extremes the coach needs to establish an effective working position, one that may have to be constantly reviewed. Oppositional logic dictates that the coach is sometimes an inspirational force, bringing out what is generous and creative in the client, but at other times is more miserly and suspicious. Perhaps this is a matter of asking a naive client 'are you being taken for a ride here?' or monitoring the progress of agreed goals, a practice that sometimes can have the same transformational effect as apparently more glamorous interventions.

What of the coach's personality biases? Again, oppositional logic is the key here. It's not that any particular personality style is necessary, so much as the ability to move between personal dimensions in response to the coachee. Sometimes the coach will need to relate to the client on his own wavelength, and at other times offer a contrarian style. For example, the coach may want to enter into the client's introvert style of being, which means being more introvert than his own personality preferences would dictate, or alternatively he may feel that modelling an extravert approach will be more helpful. Similarly, at times, a rational style will work best for a feeling-driven coachee and an emotionally expressive style with a rationally-orientated client. Being able to move across the personality spectrum and locate the right style in a session is not as complicated as it may sound and tends to develop spontaneously with experience.

The interactional coach in time and with others

Time is another dimension that throws up constant challenges for the coach who works interactionally. The very structure of coaching, with short sessions separated by long intervals of weeks or months, creates a need for temporal awareness. This is also true of the very different routes to change that exist in coaching, from the relatively straight road that leads from clarifying goals to successfully putting them into practice, to the much more winding, tortuous paths to achievement. Ultimately, there may be as many rhythms of change in coaching as there are clients, or even sessions. Learning to be open to different tempos is an art that involves staying alive to what is new, while not following it blindly. The optimal point of balance can be as elusive here as elsewhere.

Time management is also important. In a sense, the coach's ability to live in a time dimension that is less pressurized than the coachee's is a point of leverage in the coaching process. Sometimes, this can be a differentiating factor between the external and the internal coach and it is important for the external coach not to throw away this advantage through over-work.

As for the dimension of others, the coach's own interactional map can play an important role here. The network of relationships is likely to include not only the coachee but also the coaching sponsor, perhaps others in the organization and even fellow coaches, who may feature in support roles or as possible competitors. Just as the coach may ask himself where he fits into the coachee's interactional map, as a surrogate manager, for example, or a sounding board, so he should also ask what role the coachee plays in the coach's own underlying web of relationships. All coachees strike a certain chord for the coach, perhaps because they are outstandingly brilliant or energetic or because they deserve special sympathy or even pity. Whatever the particular link is to the coach's own sympathies and experience, she needs to reflect on this and its implications for the coaching relationship.

Coaching supervision

Regular supervision of the coaching process is another significant element of this interpersonal dimension, which is usually achieved through the coach's formal relationship with a qualified supervisor or a peer. The coach requires another voice – or, in the case of group supervision, several other voices – to help to explore and probe her choice consciousness. The supervision dialogue can expose aspects of the coaching relationship that the coach may not have been aware of. Everything from possible ethical issues to the professional and financial implications of particular assignments – a potential cause of anxiety sometimes omitted from discussions of supervision – can be brought to the surface in this context.

The coach as leader

Optative awareness is an essential leadership quality, and coaching may be said to relate to leadership in other respects. For example, the three stages of the choice cycle, which can be used to define leadership biases, can also help to analyse the qualities of a coach. Some coaches are natural possibilizers – comfortable in strategizing, opening up new horizons and helping the client reinterpret her situation. Other coaches may find their strengths as probabilizers, helping the client to work out accurate, realistic objectives, solve difficult practical dilemmas and build effective relationships in the organization. And some coaches are most at home in the action phase, urging a client to achievement or patiently following up on the results of an action plan.

For the interactional coach, the aim is to be comfortable in all three stages of the choice cycle. In this way, you are most able to work for the client's benefit. This means identifying your main leadership style and working on the others, in order to avoid creating an undue bias in your coaching. At the very least you should be aware of that bias and be ready to communicate it to the client, if necessary.

The interactional coach can also offer a kind of leadership in modelling open-mindedness, a proactive attitude and balancing the delivery of organizational objectives with the human reality of the workplace. This means coping as best you can with anxiety, disappointment, anger, boredom, cynicism, single-mindedness, vanity and any of the other personal and professional pitfalls to which the coach, as a human being, is prone. From time to time, it also means dealing with error, for even expert listening can falter. If the coach makes a mistake, he needs to be able to admit this without destroying his credibility.

Eight basic competences of the interactional coach

As I've suggested throughout this book, one of the main aims of the interactional approach is to unite coaching theory and coaching practice. In my view, it is probable that many of the basic competences of the interactional coach's practice are common to other coaching practices. The difference is the way the interactional model attempts to provide a consistent theoretical explanation for these competences and to integrate them with its practice across many applications. This is bound to create a different mindset for the interactional coach, which in turn will affect his or her practice.

As a useful checklist for coaches, as well as a reminder to the reader of some of the key aspects of the interactional style, let's now look at eight basic executive coaching competences in theory and practice.

Listening

Immersion in the client's situation – particularly at the beginning of every session – is crucial to understanding the client's present reality, much as phenomenology attempts to understand the world as it really is (Ihde, 1986). Expert listening means that the coach tries to manage his pre-reflective choices by avoiding pre-judgements and pre-selections and staying open to possibilities. This process also includes questioning and observation of the client and her responses to the coach's statements, whatever they may be.

Collaboration

Coaching is fundamentally a collaboration that underlines the interactional nature of reality. The coach's authentic interest in the client is the basis for working closely with him on his most desired objectives. In a competitive, high-pressure world where conflict – real and imagined – often prevails, this collaborative dialogue is especially valuable in allowing the client to clarify and implement his best possible choices.

Setting future-orientated goals

Coaching is collaboration in time, which reveals the coachee's trajectory to the future. Whether the client's goals are fixed early on or evolve during the coaching is less important than the overall process of working towards a desired future. Coaching demonstrates 'the pull' of the future and the pervasive influence of time on our lives, some-thing that the coach needs to be aware of and draw into her practice.

Maintaining confidentiality

Coaching is a response to the ultimate aloneness of human subjectivity. It offers the opportunity to explore the coachee's deepest and most controversial issues, at a personal and professional level, without fear of the conse-quences. Complete confidentiality is necessary to build up mutual trust, without which real development is impossible in coaching.

Offering learning, expertise and skills

The experience, knowledge and practical skills of the coach should never be forced on the client but offered as possible solutions, as part of the choice-making process. This includes helping the client to reinterpret her choice landscape.

Encouraging reflection and creativity

Coaching provides the ability to step back from the flurry of day-to-day events and penetrate below the surface. This involves trying to articulate unconscious dilemmas, separating real choices from mirage choices. Focusing on the possibilizing stage of the choice cycle is one reason why the coaching environment can be so creative, allowing the client to problem-solve in an innovative, risk-free atmosphere.

Providing positive and negative feedback

The coach's positive feedback provides encouragement, emotional and intellectual support and the maintenance of purpose during setbacks. This can develop confidence and reassurance and reveal new aspects of the client to himself. Constructive, and at times challenging, feedback is also crucial. The coach must be prepared to say the unsaid and speak the unspeakable, as for some executives the only negative feedback they receive is from their coach. The interactional coach is guided by the oppositional logic of positive and negative, which guards against the temptation to emphasize only one side of reality.

Encouraging the coachee to take responsibility

Ultimately the aim of coaching is to help the client take full responsibility for his choices. Although in the short term coaching may help a coachee to realize immediate goals, its long-term benefit is through the client's development of his optative awareness. This is most clearly expressed as the recognition that he is responsible for his choices and that these choices create his own identity and his contribution to the world.

Commitment to the coaching relationship

Finally, I make no apology for repeating the most important qualification for coaching interactionally, without which all the others are irrelevant, which is genuine care and concern for the well-being of the client. Coaching, to use Martin Buber's (1958) terminology, is quintessentially an 'I–You' relationship, although it is easy to get lost in the 'I–It issues' that organizations sometimes create. Even some aspects of coaching, such as the selection, monitoring and evaluation of coachees, which are intended to promote fairness and transparency, can become systematized and part of the 'it' world.

For the interactional approach the focus on the client is primary, in part because of its theoretical emphasis on the uniqueness of each human being. This means that the 'coachability' of the client (Bluckert, 2006: 34) is less of an issue than it is for some coaching models. For the interactional coach, all clients are potentially coachable and it is up to the coach to find the best way of doing this. This process is not always predictable in its outcomes, although, as we saw in the last chapter, 'success' comes in many different forms. The important thing is for the coach to be fully committed to the coaching engagement. In this way, he can help the coachee to gain an awareness of herself, her world and her way of choosing both, which will assist her in the present and stand her in good stead for the future.

References

Argyris, C. (1966) Interpersonal barriers to decision-making. *Harvard Business Review*, March–April: 84–97.

Argyris, C. & Schön, D. (1978) *Organizational Learning: A Theory of Action Perspective*. Reading, MA: Addison-Wesley.

Beck, A. (1976) *Cognitive Therapy and the Emotional Disorders*. New York: International Universities Press.

Birdwhistell, R.L. (1970) *Kinesics and Context*. Philadelphia, PA: University of Pennsylvania Press.

Bluckert, P. (2006) *Psychological Dimensions of Executive Coaching*. Maidenhead: Open University Press.

Buber, M. (1958) *I and Thou* (trans. R. Gregor Smith, revised edition). Edinburgh: T&T Clark.

Camus, A. (1955) *The Myth of Sisyphus* (trans. J. O'Brien). London: Penguin Books.

Cannon, W.B. (1931) Again the James-Lange and the thalamic theories of emotions. *Psychological Review*, 38: 83–87.

Chartered Institute of Personnel and Development (2010) *Learning and Talent Development Annual Survey Report*. London: CIPD.

Cialdini, R. (1984) *Influence: The Psychology of Persuasion*. New York: William Morrow & Co.

Cooper, C. & Palmer, S. (2000) *Conquer your Stress*. London: Chartered Institute of Personnel and Development.

Cooper, C., Cooper, R. & Eaker, L. (1988) *Living with Stress*. London: Penguin Books.

Corrie, S. & Lane, D. (2009) The scientist-practitioner model as a framework for coaching psychology. *The Coaching Psychologist*, 5(2): 61–67.

Costa, P. & McCrea, R. (2003) *Personality in Adulthood: A Five-Factor Theory Perspective*. New York: Guilford Press.

Csikszentmihalyi, M. (1975) *Beyond Boredom and Anxiety*. San Francisco, CA: Jossey-Bass.

De Haan, E. (2008) *Relational Coaching: Journeys Towards Mastering One-to-One Learning*. Chichester: John Wiley.

Eliot, G. (1995) *Daniel Deronda*. London: Penguin Books.

Eliot, T.S. (1941) *Burnt Norton*. London: Faber & Faber.

Empson, W. (1930) Seven *Types of Ambiguity*. London: Chatto & Windus.

Forster, E.M. (1910) *Howards End*. London: Edward Arnold.

Freud, S. (1963) *Introductory Lectures on Psychoanalysis*. London: Hogarth Press.

Gadamer, H.-G. (1975) *Truth and Method* (trans. J. Weinsheimer & D. Marshall). London: Sheed & Ward.

Gardner, H. (1983) *Frames of Mind: The Theory of Multiple Intelligences*. New York: Basic Books.

Glietman, H., Gross J. & Reisberg D. (2010) *Psychology* (8th edition). New York: Norton.

Goffman, E. (1959) *The Presentation of Self in Everyday Life*. Edinburgh: University of Edinburgh Social Sciences Research Centre.

Goleman, D. (1995) *Emotional Intelligence*. New York: Bantam Books.

Goleman, D., Boyatzis, R. & McKee, A. (2002) *Primal Leadership: Realizing the Power of Emotional Intelligence*. Cambridge, MA: Harvard Business School Press.

Green, S. (1994) *Principles of Biopsychology*. Hove, UK: Lawrence Erlbaum Associates.

Greene, J. & Grant, A. (2003) *Solution-Focused Coaching: Managing People in a Complex World*. Harlow: Pearson.

Hammond, J., Keeny, R. & Raiffa, H. (1989) A rational method for making trade-offs. *Harvard Business Review*, March–April: 137–149.

Hampden-Turner, C. (1994) Corporate *Culture: How to Generate Organisational Strength and Lasting Commercial Advantage*. London: Piatkus.

Hegel, G.W.F. (1931) *The Phenomenology of Mind* (trans. J.B. Baillie). London: Macmillan.

Heidegger, M. (1962) *Being and Time* (trans. J. Macquarrie & E. Robinson). Oxford: Blackwell.

Heidegger, M. (2001) *Zollikon Seminars: Protocols–Conversations–Letters* (trans. F. Mayr & R. Askay). Evanston, IL: Northwestern University Press.

Heter, T. (2006) Authenticity and others: Sartre's ethics of recognition. *Sartre Studies International*, 12(2): 17–43.

Husserl, E. (1931) *Ideas: General Introduction to Pure Phenomenology* (trans. W.R. Boyce Gibson). London: George Allen.

Ihde, D. (1986) *Experimental Phenomenology: An Introduction*. New York: Putnam.

Jacobsen, B. (2007) *Invitation to Existential Psychology: A Psychology for the Unique Human Being and its Applications in Therapy*. Chichester: John Wiley.

James, W. (1890) *The Principles of Psychology*, Volume 2. New York: Henry Holt.

Joseph, S. & Bryant-Jeffries, R. (2009) Person-centred coaching psychology. In S. Palmer & A. Whybrow (eds.), *Handbook of Coaching Psychology: A Guide for Practitioners*. London: Routledge.

Katsenelinboigen, A. (1997) *The Concept of Indeterminism and its Applications: Economics, Social Systems, Ethics, Artificial Intelligence and Aesthetics*. Westport, CT: Praeger.

Kierkegaard, S. (1980) *The Concept of Anxiety* (trans. R. Thomte). Princeton, NJ: Princeton University Press.

Kierkegaard, S. (1992) *Either/Or: A Fragment of Life* (trans. A. Hannay). London: Penguin Books.

Kierkegaard, S. (1996) *Papers and Journals: A Selection* (trans. A. Hannay). London: Penguin Books.

Kierkegaard, S. (2000) Johannes Climacus, or *De omnibus dubitandum est*. In H. Hong & E. Hong (eds.), *The Essential Kierkegaard*. Princeton, NJ: Princeton University Press.

Kotter, J. (1996) *Leading Change*. Boston, MA: Harvard Business School Press.

Laing, R.D. (1960) *The Divided Self: An Existential Study in Sanity and Madness*. London: Penguin Books.

Lao-Tsu (1993) *Tao Te Ching* (trans. S Aldiss & S. Lombardo). Indianapolis, IN: Hackett Publishing.

Lazarus, A. (1981) *The Practice of Multimodal Therapy*. New York: McGraw-Hill.

Lee, G. (2003) *Leadership Coaching: From Personal Insight to Organisational Performance*. London: Chartered Institute of Personnel and Development.

Leimon, A., Moscovici, F. & McMahon, G. (2005) *Essential Business Coaching*. London: Routledge.

Linley, A. & Harrington, S. (2009) Integrating positive psychology and coaching psychology: Shared assumptions and aspirations?

In S. Palmer & A. Whybrow (eds.), *Handbook of Coaching Psychology: A Guide for Practitioners*. London: Routledge.

Locke, E. & Latham, G. (1990) *A Theory of Goal-Setting and Task Performance*. Englewood Cliffs, NJ: Prentice-Hall.

Ludeman, K. & Erlandson, E. (2004) Coaching the alpha male. *Harvard Business Review*, 82: 58–67.

May, R. (1969) *Love and Will*. New York: Norton.

May, R. (1977) *The Meaning of Anxiety* (revised edition). New York: Norton.

Merleau-Ponty, M. (1962) *The Phenomenology of Perception* (trans. C. Smith). London: Routledge.

Merleau-Ponty, M. (1974) Indirect language and the voices of silence. In *Phenomenology, Language and Sociology: Selected Essays of Maurice Merleau-Ponty* (trans. J. O'Neill). London: Heinemann.

Mintzberg, H. (1990) The manager's job: Folklore and fact. *Harvard Business Review*, March–April: 163–178.

Neenan, M. (2006) Cognitive behavioural coaching. In J. Passmore (ed.), *Excellence in Coaching: The Industry Guide*. London: Kogan Page.

Orenstein, R. (2007) *Multi-Dimensional Executive Coaching*. New York: Springer.

Orwell, G. (1945) *Animal Farm*. London: Martin Secker & Warburg.

Palmer, S. & Szymanska, K. (2009) Cognitive behavioural coaching: An integrative approach. In S. Palmer and A. Whybrow (eds.), *Handbook of Coaching Psychology: A Guide for Practitioners*. London: Routledge.

Peltier, B. (2001) *The Psychology of Executive Coaching: Theory and Application*. New York: Brunner-Routledge.

Prochaska, J., Norcross, J. & Diclemente, C. (2006) *Changing for Good*. New York: Collins.

Sartre, J.-P. (1948) *Existentialism and Humanism* (trans. P. Mairet). London: Methuen Library.

Sartre, J.-P. (1958) *Being and Nothingness: An Essay on Phenomenological Ontology* (trans. H. Barnes). London: Routledge.

Sartre, J.-P. (1992) *Notebooks for an Ethics* (trans. D. Pellauer). Chicago: University of Chicago Press.

Satir, V. (1967) *Conjoint Family Therapy: A Guide to Theory and Technique*. Palo Alto, CA: Science and Behaviour Books.

Shaw, P. & Linnecar, R. (2007) *Business Coaching: Achieving Practical Results Through Effective Engagement*. Chichester: Capstone.

Smith, J. & Holland, T. (1987) *EastEnders: The Inside Story*. London: BBC Books.

Spinelli, E. (1989) *The Interpreted World: An Introduction to Phenomenological Psychology*. London: Sage Publications.

Spinelli, E. (2010) Existential coaching. In E. Cox, T. Bachkirova & D. Clutterbuck (eds.), *The Complete Handbook of Coaching*. London: Sage Publications.

Spinelli, E. & Horner, C. (2009) An existential approach to coaching psychology. In S. Palmer & A. Whybrow (eds.), *Handbook of Coaching Psychology: A Guide for Practitioners*. London: Routledge.

Stanislavski, C. (1937) *An Actor Prepares*. London: Geoffrey Bles.

Stein, G. (1922) *Geography and Plays*. Boston, MA: The Four Seas Company.

Tappin, S. & Cave, A. (2008) *The Secrets of CEOs: 150 Global Chief Executives Lift the Lid on Business, Life and Leadership*. London: Nicholas Brealey.

Van Deurzen-Smith, E. (1988) *Existential Counselling in Practice*. London: Sage Publications.

Voltaire (2005) *Candide, or Optimism* (trans. T. Cuffe). London: Penguin Books.

Wason, P. (1960) On the failure to eliminate hypotheses in a conceptual task. *Quarterly Journal of Experimental Psychology*, 12(3): 129–140.

Whybrow, A. & Palmer, S. (2006) Taking stock: A survey of coaching psychologists' practices and perspectives. *International Coaching Psychology Review*, 1(1): 56–70.

Yalom, I. (1980) *Existential Psychotherapy*. New York: Basic Books.

Yalom, I. (1989) *Love's Executioner and Other Tales of Psychotherapy*. London: Penguin Books.

Taylor & Francis

eBooks

FOR LIBRARIES

ORDER YOUR
FREE 30 DAY
INSTITUTIONAL
TRIAL TODAY!

Over 23,000 eBook titles in the Humanities,
Social Sciences, STM and Law from some of the
world's leading imprints.

Choose from a range of subject packages or create your own!

Benefits for **you**

▶ Free MARC records
▶ COUNTER-compliant usage statistics
▶ Flexible purchase and pricing options

Benefits for your **user**

▶ Off-site, anytime access via Athens or referring URL
▶ Print or copy pages or chapters
▶ Full content search
▶ Bookmark, highlight and annotate text
▶ Access to thousands of pages of quality research
   at the click of a button

For more information, pricing enquiries or to order
a free trial, contact your local online sales team.

UK and Rest of World: **online.sales@tandf.co.uk**

US, Canada and Latin America:
e-reference@taylorandfrancis.com

www.ebooksubscriptions.com

ALPSP Award for
BEST eBOOK
PUBLISHER
2009 Finalist

Taylor & Francis eBooks
Taylor & Francis Group

A flexible and dynamic resource for teaching, learning and research.